S0-ABD-716

"Once again, Dr. Lew Losoncy has captured the essence of a dynamic concept...this time introducing the attitude component of self-help psychology as a nutritional science. Plus, he gives us a simple road map to follow to grow ourself."

Mike DeGennaro
President, Matrix Essentials

"Practical...TODAY is filled with lots of activities that anyone can go out and think/feel and do to change their life. Right now. TODAY! Invaluable...I found the inclusion of thinking/doing/feeling extremely valuable. The book is one of the few to offer a comprehensive way to change, rather than a piecemeal approach that is so popular. I was able to identify my own style and then use the very practical activities in TODAY to get started right away."

James Belasco, Ph.D.
Professor of Management, San Diego State University
Author, "Teaching an Elephant to Dance" & "Flight of the Buffalo"

"Losoncy helps you today to change your life. You can learn your dominant attitude style. The exercises presented help initiate change in your thoughts, feelings and actions. TODAY will give you courage for tomorrow!"

Dr. Don Dinkmeyer
Co-author of "Systematic Training for Effective Parenting (STEP)"

"How many times have you said, 'I'll start my new program on Monday,' and Monday never arrived? Procrastination is the fruit of ignorance. TODAY is the beginning of mastering your destiny. Dr. Lew Losoncy has effectively defined life in its most simplest terms. TODAY...a real winner!"

Bob Arriaga
General Manager
Melbourne Athletic Club

"If you have tried and failed to break a habit, instead of giving up, read the Breakthrough Chapter of TODAY and you will find an approach that will work — if you use it. You were too busy trying to change your thinking, or your feelings, or your actions, instead of changing your total attitude. But don't do what you have been doing for too long...putting it off until tomorrow. Do it TODAY!"

George Vogel, M.Ed.
Executive Director, Council on Chemical Abuse
Berks County, Pennsylvania

"Educators and their students will find that TODAY! is a recipe for living. Dr. Losoncy's ingredients provide a logical and realistic approach to finding inner strength and fulfillment. You have heard about empowering yourself and others. This book shows you step by step how to empower."

Linda Anderson, M.Ed.
Director of Guidance and Counseling
Satellite Beach High School, Florida

TODAY!

GRAB IT

7 Vital *Attitude* Nutrients
to Build the New You

TODAY!

GRAB IT

7 Vital Attitude Nutrients to Build the New You

Dr. Lewis Losoncy

St. Lucie Press
Boca Raton   Boston   New York   Washington, D.C.   London

Artwork provided by Matrix Essentials
                     30601 Carter Street
                     Solon, OH 44139
                     216-248-3700

Project Editor: Sandy Pearlman
Compositor: Roy Barnhill
Cover Design: Denise Craig
Manufacturing: Barbara Brownlee

Library of Congress Cataloging-in-Publication Data

Catalog information may be obtained from the Library of Congress

This book contains information obtained from authentic and highly regarded sources. Reprinted material is quoted with permission, and sources are indicated. A wide variety of references are listed. Reasonable efforts have been made to publish reliable data and information, but the author and the publisher cannot assume responsibility for the validity of all materials or for the consequences of their use.

Neither this book nor any part may be reproduced or transmitted in any form or by any means, electronic or mechanical, including photocopying, microfilming, and recording, or by any information storage or retrieval system, without prior permission in writing from the publisher.

The consent of CRC Press LLC does not extend to copying for general distribution, for promotion, for creating new works, or for resale. Specific permission must be obtained in writing from CRC Press LLC for such copying.

Direct all inquiries to CRC Press LLC, 2000 Corporate Blvd., N.W., Boca Raton, Florida 33431.

Trademark Notice: Product or corporate names may be trademarks or registered trademarks, and are used only for identification and explanation, without intent to infringe.

© 1998 by CRC Press LLC
St. Lucie Press is an imprint of CRC Press LLC

No claim to original U.S. Government works
International Standard Book Number 1-57444-213-9
Printed in the United States of America 1 2 3 4 5 6 7 8 9 0
Printed on acid-free paper

Yesterday's Endings Are Seeds
for TODAY'S Beginnings

Endings are seeds for beginnings.
Tomorrow will come — in time.
Even in hopelessness lies a seed of hope,
And even a small seed can climb!

But the little seed has to give up its past
on its voyage to the sprouting tree.
Didn't you ever transcend in your life,
Previous visions of who you could be?

Every cloud opens up to the smiling sun
And the low will soon reach high tide.
Exits and entrances are at the same gate;
Moving through "what was" is your ticket to pride.

Two triangles have to surrender themselves
To ever make it to the square.
And every simple discovery in life
Makes you give up something you swore was there.

Yes, you have to give up your known discomfort
In order for you to soar in flight.
But isn't the end of something that's wrong
the beginning of something that's right?

TODAY you stand at the place where endings meet beginnings,
Deciding your fate — handcuffed or free.
One path will take you to the place you have been;
The other is the seed to lift you to where you want to be.

So pick yourself up like the bright rising sun,
Like the wind lifting the silent sea.
But hope in your heart like that seedling in spring
And go forward. TODAY. And design your new destiny!

Lewis Losoncy

DEDICATION

To Gabrielle, who, at six, goes forward
with the courage of a lion, and the sensitivity of a lullaby

To my wife, Diane, who I see more beautiful each day

To Arnie Miller, for elevating a profession

To Sydell Miller, our friend, whose strength and heart
give courage to anyone who has ever met her

To Albert Ellis, the most significant influence
on psychotherapy today and our family's friend
and attitude nutrient source

To Don Dinkmeyer, the highest compliment,
our encourager

To Bruce J. Thomas, the universal archetype
of a family physician

To Madison Smith and Marnee McClellan,
for their friendship

And to the worldwide community of beauty professionals
who provide New Attitude Nutrients to cosmetically
and psychologically transform self-images and destinies
of fellow human beings!

TABLE OF CONTENTS

℞: PURPOSE & PASSION Nutrient
- ✔ Nutrient to find meaning and create dreams, goals, success (Thought)
- ✔ Nutrient for enthusiasm, high spirits, desire for achievement (Feeling)
- ✔ Nutrient to take action and reach dreams (Action)

℞: INNER SECURITY Nutrient
- ✔ Nutrient to affirm inner assets, strengths and resources to succeed (Thought)
- ✔ Nutrient for security, self-confidence, self-reliance, inner knowing (Feeling)
- ✔ Nutrient to take self-determined action, without outside support (Action)

"Today, I'll condition myself to immediately accept anything I can't change!"

℞: **ACCEPTANCE Nutrient**
- ✔ Nutrient to accept "what is, is," to focus energies constructively (Thought)
- ✔ Nutrient for acceptance, joy, serenity, calmness, peace, relaxation (Feeling)
- ✔ Nutrient to take action and "let go" or "let it be" (Action)

"Today, I'll proceed with understanding rather than judgment toward others!"

℞: **UNDERSTANDING Nutrient**
- ✔ Nutrient to understand, rather than judge, to improve relationships and effectiveness with others (Thought)
- ✔ Nutrient for understanding, empathy, sensitivity, caring (Feeling)
- ✔ Nutrient to take action, using successful understanding skills (Action)

"Today, I'll courageously go through my anxieties and fears!"

℞: **COURAGE Nutrient**
- ✔ Nutrient to bust through anxieties, fears and enter your New Attitude Growth Zone (Thought)
- ✔ Nutrient for courage, strength, will-ingness (Feeling)
- ✔ Nutrient to take action and move forward into the rich unknown possibilities (Action)

℞: INSPIRATION Nutrient
- ✔ Nutrient to transcend ego, find universal, not selfish, perspective (Thought)
- ✔ Nutrient for inspiration, energy, expansion, positive motivation (Feeling)
- ✔ Nutrient to take action with universal base (Action)

℞: LEADERSHIP Nutrient
- ✔ Nutrient to communicate respect and vision and encourage buy-in (Thought)
- ✔ Nutrient for confidence, optimism and high energy (Feeling)
- ✔ Nutrient to motivate others to unite and to move toward goals (Action)

ACKNOWLEDGMENTS

Thank you to every one of my special teammates at Matrix Essentials. We changed the world together because we cared to protect, preserve and enhance the integrity of a profession!

Thank you to Matrix's distributorship network and sales force who are helping to elevate a profession of people!

Thank you to Mike DeGennaro for his integrity to carry on a dream for a profession of a million plus, to my eternal friend Sara Jones, and to my talented colleagues Jim Fisher, Bob Goehrke, Jeff Schwartz, Robert Bednar, Randy Markey, Tony Beckerman, Mike Nitschke, R. W. Miller, Ron Beible, Penney Parker, Rod Kyriakiades, Julie Sleva, Shelly Smith, Ginny Guinn, Debbie Lyerly, Frances Shunick, Jayne Peterson, Piet Loomans and Aaron Graham for their help with *TODAY!* Thanks to Deborah Lee and Charlene Kleinke for their contribution to *TODAY!* Also to Sherry DeGennaro for her important vital, timely decision governing this book.

To the worldwide influences of my friends Ricardo, Catherine and Tony Altieri, Vivienne Mackinder, Luis Alvarez, Nicholas French, Heidimarie Hisle, Philadelphia Joe Santy, Dennis Millard, Tom Reid, and Donn and Leilani Matlock for our thought-provoking conversations that influenced this developing manuscript.

To my teammates, Elaine Cressman, Don Wismer, Annette Moore, Cindy O'Neal and Chris Kuhen. Major thanks also to Robin Olson, who is always there to get the job done!

To the awesome team at St. Lucie Press, especially to Dennis Buda, simply a genius. To Dennis McClellan, who could play all nine positions on a publishing team at once and be an all-star at each one. He found a way against all odds. To Sandy Pearlman, the best there is at editing in the known universe. To Drew Gierman, Carolyn Lea, Becky McEldowney, Jonathan Pennell, Denise Craig and Roy Barnhill, the Boca deadline quota busters! Any author would find it a dream working with this talented, motivated team.

ABOUT THE AUTHOR

Lewis Losoncy is the author of fifteen books on encouragement, success and teamwork. He is also the psychologist for Matrix Essentials in Solon, Ohio, North America's largest producer of professional beauty products.

He is the author of *The Best Team Skills, The Motivating Team Leader, The Skills of Encouragement* (with Don Dinkmeyer) and *What Is, Is!* (with Diane Losoncy).

Dr. Losoncy has appeared on CNN, "CBS This Morning" and in varied print media, from *Psychology Today* to *Prevention Magazine* to *The Wall Street Journal*. He has spoken in all fifty U.S. states and throughout Canada, Australia and New Zealand.

"Dr. Lew" lives in Indialantic, Florida, with his wife, Diane, and his daughter, Gabrielle Anna.

Symptoms Inhibiting Growth Today & Recommended New Attitude Nutrients

Anger at life .... #3   **Acceptance Nutrient**
Anger at others .... #4   **Understanding Nutrient**
Anxiety .... #5   **Courage Nutrient**
Apathy .... #1   **Purpose & Passion Nutrient**
Approval needs .... #2   **Inner Security Nutrient**
Blaming .... #3   **Acceptance Nutrient**
Burnout .... #1   **Purpose & Passion Nutrient**
Co-dependency .... #2   **Inner Security Nutrient**
Creative blockage .... #6   **Inspiration Nutrient**
Decision-making difficulties .... #7   **Leadership Nutrient**
Defensiveness .... #6   **Inspiration Nutrient**
Dependency .... #2   **Inner Security Nutrient**
Discouragement .... #5   **Courage Nutrient**
Fears (e.g., public speaking) .... #5   **Courage Nutrient**
Feelings of rejection .... #2   **Inner Security Nutrient**
Jealousy .... #2   **Inner Security Nutrient**
Helplessness .... #7   **Leadership Nutrient**
Inferiority feelings .... #7   **Leadership Nutrient**
Living in the past .... #3   **Acceptance Nutrient**
Living in a rut, depression .... #1   **Purpose & Passion Nutrient**
Loss of confidence .... #2   **Inner Security Nutrient**
Loss of passion .... #1   **Purpose & Passion Nutrient**
Mid-life crisis .... #1   **Purpose & Passion Nutrient**
Overperfectionism .... #5   **Courage Nutrient**
Pessimism .... #6   **Inspiration Nutrient**
Problem handling criticism .... #6   **Inspiration Nutrient**
Relationship problems .... #4   **Understanding Nutrient**
Resentment .... #4   **Understanding Nutrient**
Sadness .... #6   **Inspiration Nutrient**
Shyness .... #7   **Leadership Nutrient**
Stressed out .... #3   **Acceptance Nutrient**
Worries .... #5   **Courage Nutrient**

INTRODUCTION

Being alive sure gives us some options, doesn't it? Two of our options include enjoying or fighting the experiences of our life. Our happiness and success pretty much rest on our attitude, don't they? The interesting thing is that in our whole lifetime of about 30,000 days, we have only one day in which we have any power. And that day is *TODAY!* When my attitude *TODAY* dwells on reliving yesterday, I lose all of the potential progress power present right in front of me now. And when my attitude *TODAY* is to push off making the needed improvements in my life until tomorrow, I make two major mistakes.

First, I erroneously conclude that, somehow or other, change will be easier to create tomorrow. In reality, a new attitude, which means new thoughts, feelings and actions, will be harder to build later, because I will be older. Plus, in the meantime, I will be psychologically burdened by making these changes a thousand times in my mind, and then I am still faced with making the change anyway. I could avoid doing it over and over again those thousand times in my mind by taking acting *TODAY!* And then my mind is freed to create fulfillment.

A second error I make in deciding to change my life later is that I fool myself, because tomorrow never really comes. The only real moment I have is *TODAY.* The only thing I will ever have is *TODAY.* If something is going to happen to improve my life, I have to make a commitment, and take action, *TODAY!* It always works when I do, doesn't it?

"TODAY!" is my best chance to change my life. But where do I start? Where can I find the inner strength to supplement my change to go forward? What in me do I change first?

"TODAY!" is designed to provide attitude nutrients to help you:

- ✔ Make those changes that you have been thinking about for some time
- ✔ Create new dreams for your todays of tomorrow
- ✔ Get started *TODAY!* In fact, you can get started NOW!

To start growing from these recently discovered attitude nutrients, it is important to understand the importance of attitude in one's life.

If the food you eat provides the nutrients to grow you a healthy body, what would be the equivalent nutrients to grow you a healthy attitude?

How much time in your life have you spent thinking about providing the right nutritious diet for your body? How much time have you spent thinking about providing yourself the right vital nutrients for your mind, heart and spirit?

Do you believe that your physical body is much more important than your attitude?

Or do you believe that your mind, heart and spirit, like your physical self, need nutrients to keep them growing and renewed — but you just don't know where to find nutrients for your deeper self?

That's where New Attitude Nutrients come into play. New Attitude Nutrients are designed to build you at the very center of your self-control. Your fundamental you is your attitude, that is, your thoughts, feelings and actions toward yourself, others and life. Everything you experience in life flows from your inner attitude, doesn't it? And your outer world starts changing the very instant your inner attitude changes. With New Attitude Nutrients, your attitude evolves from "Some day, my life will get better" to "Today, I am going to change my life!"

In fact, the single most vital and consequential influence on your fulfillment in life is your attitude. A new attitude gives you a new life. Immediately!

New Attitude Nutrients provide you a simple and unique approach to growing your thoughts, your feelings and your very actions in life. With these 7 New Attitude Nutrients, you will be:

1.   Finding a deeper purpose and igniting your passion for life (PURPOSE & PASSION Nutrient)
2.   Moving from environmental dependency to inner security (INNER SECURITY Nutrient)
3.   Rising above frustration to immediately accept that "What is, is!" (ACCEPTANCE Nutrient)
4.   Freeing your personal growth energies by understanding others, rather than consuming your energies judging others (UNDERSTANDING Nutrient)
5.   Developing your courage to be imperfect, to face the unknown and to break through your fears and anxieties in order to move from your Comfort Rut Zone to your New Attitude Growth Zone (COURAGE Nutrient)
6.   Transcending a narrow, selfish, defensive ego and living from your universal energetic spirit (INSPIRATION Nutrient)
7.   Promoting yourself to being the leader of your life — determining your own destiny — while encouraging others to grow with you (LEADERSHIP Nutrient)

The major uniqueness of New Attitude Nutrients is that these attitude supplements can be quickly grasped, mastered and taught. After reading the chapter on "The Breakthrough of New Attitude Nutrients," you will fully understand *how* and *why* New Attitude Nutrients are different. The balance of your attitude nutrient program will teach you *what to do* to grow through the resources offered by the 7 New Attitude Nutrients.

New Attitude Nutrients focus on total attitude change. You will find yourself growing in all three vital components of your attitude, that is, your (1) thoughts, (2) feelings and (3) actions.

Think of it: If previous personal growth approaches failed, wasn't it because only one of those three parts of your total attitude was changed? And the other two-thirds of your attitude were not moved!

New Attitude Nutrients are also unique in that they are produced to affect all three areas of your total attitude by starting with your Dominant Attitude Style. You will soon learn your own personal Dominant Attitude Style and its arrangement. Proceeding from your own unique style is the most comfortable and effective way to acquire your 7 New Attitude Nutrients.

YOU ARE ON THE CONSTRUCTION SITE FOR YOUR NEW ATTITUDE. *TODAY!*

Imagine yourself on the most important construction site of your life — the building of your new attitude!

New Attitude Nutrients can't build a great building, but they can build the builder of that great building. You!

New Attitude Nutrients can't build that great work of art, but they can help build the builder of that great work of art. You!

And New Attitude Nutrients can't build your world-changing dream, but they can build the dreamer of that dream. You!

Waiting for your world to change before you change is like looking at your reflection in the mirror and saying, "You move first. Then I'll move." A more nutritional approach is to look into the mirror at your reflection and say, "I'll move first, then I can guarantee you will move."

Stop waiting. Start growing! Grow your inner sources over your challenging forces, powered by an attitude nourished with New Attitude Nutrients.

Because *TODAY* is your best chance to change your life!

THE BREAKTHROUGH OF NEW ATTITUDE NUTRIENTS:

Philosophy, Description and Directions for Usage

NOW Is the Only Moment with Any Power in My Life!

We have about two billion five hundred million seconds of life in our body form. In each of these two and one-half billion instants we have a tremendous range of potential sadness or happiness, failure or success. And the quality of our whole lifetime rests on whether we are functioning optimally or minimally in each of these vital moments. Each fleeting moment has the potential for success only once; then it moves on — lost forever, never to be recaptured. When the instant is experienced fully and used wisely, with all of our inner creative strength and power, we not only enhance that moment, but we add resources to our coping tool kit to be used later.

The cartoon character Pogo concluded, "We have met the enemy, and he is us!" So true, isn't it? Sometimes we actually use our own resource, our unlimited creative mind, against ourselves, building up our challenges and, worse still, then tearing ourselves down. Every time we put ourselves down, it's like consciously passing a football into the arms of our challenge in life. Imagine! So many moments are lost, consumed in negative, hopeless thinking, destructive or painful emotions, inaction and missed opportunities.

For example, when we relive the past rather than grab hold of the power of the present, we miss the precious moment, consumed by what was, thereby forfeiting our potential happiness and success as "now" passes us by, unnoticed. We have only one moment in life where we have any power. And that moment is now! Imagine using the power of now by reliving what was! When we live in the past, we feel hopeless because we can't change it. Worse, we may conclude that life in general is hopeless, because we can't change what was! We need some attitude nutrients to help us realize that just because we can't change what was doesn't mean we can't change what is or design what will be!

Consider seven vital choices we make each day — each moment — that weaken, put down or even destroy our growth potential, while at the same time building up our inner and outer challenges:

1. Choosing to proceed today without some purpose and some passion for our life, our day and our moment in time, we find ourselves apathetic and lacking a reason for this moment in time. Without a point to aim at, or a destination to reach, our life is aimless, pointless and our destiny is determined by something other than ourselves, like fate, luck or chance! No wonder we feel helpless! By taking the New Attitude Nutrient of PURPOSE & PASSION, we find a mission, a reason, and fire it up with energy and enthusiasm — while we still have it! Seize this moment!

2. Choosing to blame the world for where we are today only serves to make our opponent stronger, because we give our power to whatever we are blaming. It is the thing controlling our life, because we can't change unless "it" changes. Think about it. If you are making your happiness and success depend upon somebody else changing, you are dooming yourself to helplessness, dependency or co-dependency for the rest of your life. How long have you been waiting for "it," or "them," to change? How much longer will you wait, before you take your own action in your life? Stop giving your power away! Stop blaming and start growing. The surest way — from the inside out! Take the New Attitude

Nutrient of INNER SECURITY and build your own self-determination. Your outer environment will change constantly in life, but you will always have you!

3. Choosing to dwell on the things we won't or can't change only frustrates us, weakening us and strengthening our opponent, our challenge in life. If there is anything about your past that has been consuming your energies, let go — now! Take the New Attitude Nutrient of ACCEPTANCE and tell yourself firmly, "What is, is!" In addition, condition yourself to immediately and serenely accept anything you aren't going to change. And then, move your new attitude forward full force against your real challenges in life. And change them! Begin now!

4. Choosing to judge people, rather than to understand them, results in making us totally ineffective with others and also creates tensions in our relationships. Tensions drain our valuable energies that could be used to change our life. To be happy in life, it certainly helps to have the attitudes and skills to be successful with others. By taking the New Attitude Nutrient of UNDERSTANDING, we immediately will find its effects taking place, enriching our communications and connections with people. Understanding also earns us a position of influence in other people's lives. Judging preaches to others; understanding teaches us and them.

5. Choosing to be held back by our anxieties and fears imprisons us in our Comfort Rut Zone for life. The future will look exactly as today looks, except we will be much older. Take the New Attitude Nutrient of COURAGE, and bust through your comfort zone and enter your New Attitude Growth Zone. Hasn't every great moment in your life been a moment in which you went beyond your anxieties and found both refreshment and strength?

6. Choosing to be caught up defending our limited, selfish, tired ego, rather than drawing from our universal, creative energies of essential spirit, blocks our spontaneity. We lose those moments, in defense, rather than in creation. When your ego gets caught up in the trap of prestige and approval in the eyes of others, you are manipulated by your perception of how others perceive you. You are dependent upon what others think of you. Take the New Attitude Nutrient of INSPIRATION and expand yourself through universal strength.

7. Choosing to live in hope that someone else will make our world, our family, our job or neighborhood a better place doesn't work. Take the LEADER-SHIP Nutrient, and you will be the one to change your world. This is the surest way to make things happen!

How many moments have we already lost out of our two billion plus? How many more moments could we lose? How much would it be worth for us to find more pleasure, fulfillment and success in each of our remaining moments? Can you make a commitment for a few hours to strengthen yourself with New Attitude Nutrients?

PHILOSOPHICAL SOURCE OF NEW ATTITUDE NUTRIENTS: ALBERT ELLIS'S RATIONAL EMOTIVE BEHAVIOR THERAPY

Many practicing psychotherapists and counselors today would agree that their approach to clients has been strongly influenced by the philosophy and the ideas of New York City psychologist Albert Ellis. Ellis challenged his psychoanalytic training because of some unsound generalizations about the inevitable helplessness people feel, overwhelmed by their unconscious, biological, childhood sexual forces. His original system of rational thinking, outlined in *Reason and Emotion in Psychotherapy* (1973), showed how it wasn't a person's past but a person's view of his or her past that continues to upset and disturb the person emotionally. Our thinking about our past, not our past itself, is the culprit, Ellis concluded in his bestseller, *A New Guide to Rational Living* (1975). Change your thinking, and you change your feelings about your past. After all, our past doesn't touch us directly, but rather indirectly through our cognitive processes. Isn't that why two people with the same past have two different reactions to it?

Stop and think about Ellis's observation for a minute. Is it possible that it's not what happened to us but rather what we keep telling ourselves (our thoughts) about what happened to us that continues to disturb us today? Can you feel the nutrients in Ellis's brilliant, empowering observation? Millions of people throughout the world do.

The most amazing fact about Ellis, America's leading thinker on psychotherapy, is that, at almost age eighty, the open-minded theorist and practitioner, guided only by scientific accuracy, saw an inaccuracy in the name of his system of almost half a century. In *The Behavior Therapist* (1993), Ellis wrote:

> *Why have I decided, after almost 40 years of creating and using rational emotive therapy* RET, *to change its name to rational emotive behavior therapy* (REBT)? *Mainly because, I can see now that I was wrong to call it, for a few years, rational therapy* (RT), *and then, in 1961, to change it to* RET.
>
> *...So, to correct my previous errors and to set the record straight, I shall from now on call it what it has really always been — rational emotive behavior therapy* (REBT).

Ellis's 1993 insight and, as importantly, his principles, which since the 1950s have emphasized changing all three components — a person's thoughts, feelings and behaviors, were, to me, the creative source of New Attitude Nutrients.

I am not alone. Name any popular psychologist today, and you will find Ellis's insights buried in his or her thoughts and words.

It was Ellis who first saw, in 1955, that to change, we need to change three components — our thoughts, our feelings and our behaviors — which leads us to New Attitude Nutrients.

Let's take a few minutes to examine how rational emotive behavior therapy and New Attitude Nutrients differ from many other systems of change.

New Attitude Nutrients emerged from the observation that almost all approaches to cognitive (thinking), emotive or behavioral change work some of the time, but not all of the time.

For example, perhaps you have tried motivation, personal growth, behavior change or self-help approaches before and found them effective. Or maybe you committed to them and gave up, or perhaps their effects didn't seem to last long. Let's analyze why personal growth approaches work or don't work.

First of all, when an approach is effective, it is likely due to the fact that *the approach changes your total attitude*, that is, your (1) thoughts, (2) feelings and (3) actions. On the other hand, when a system doesn't work, it is likely due to the fact that it enriches only one of these three aspects of your attitude.

Maybe you experienced a personal growth approach that focused on changing your thinking. Some very effective personal growth approaches center on your thoughts, your view and changing your beliefs. Change your thinking, and you change your life! Thought modification is vital, but if the system changed only your thoughts and didn't change your feelings, and there was no resultant change in your actual behaviors in life, then the approach didn't change your total attitude.

Maybe you went to an uplifting motivation seminar and felt immediately lifted emotionally. In this instance, the focus again was on one-third of your attitude, your feelings. If the program moved you to change your thoughts and your actions in life, it was effective. If not, and only your feelings changed, your motivation probably faded within a week.

Maybe you used behavior modification and positive reinforcement. You may have drawn up charts, graphs and rewards for your new behaviors. It might have been very effective if your thoughts and feelings also changed. Or perhaps it became boring, because your feelings and thinking were not engaged. Your actions and behaviors are the focus in a behaviorally focused system. This approach is often effective when your thoughts and feelings are modified as well.

In other words, *for a total attitude change to occur, all of your attitude components — your thoughts, your feelings and your actual behaviors — must be touched, moved and changed.*

A second reason why a personal growth approach may not have worked is because you were almost immediately turned off. Why would a system not make sense, not feel right or turn you off in the beginning? Well, *if a total attitude transformation is going to occur, and produce meaningful and long-lasting change for you, its most effective starting point is with your Dominant Attitude Style.* Your Dominant Attitude Style is the initiation point of your attitude modification. You could be a Think-er, a Feel-er or a Do-er. To effectively change your total attitude, that is, your (1) thoughts, (2) feelings and (3) actions, you start with your dominant style. You will have a chance to assess your Dominant Attitude Style shortly, and this will surely give you information that will help you in all aspects of your life.

Let's explore a practical and positive way of looking at your life that will set the stage for acquiring your New Attitude Nutrients.

OUR LIFE CHALLENGES ARE INSIDE, NOT OUTSIDE US

There are two major attitudes we can take toward our life challenges. Think of a challenge you face today. Now consider your perception of the relative strength of your inner resources against your perception of your challenge. Which of the following best describes your attitude today?

Does it look like this:

My perception of my inner resources

vs.

My Perception of My Outer Challenge

Or, does it look like this:

My Perception of My Inner Resources

vs.

My perception of my outer challenge

We have just compared our perception of the strength of our inner resources versus our perception of the strength of our outer challenge. Our attitude goes to the vital heart of the New Attitude Nutrient philosophy. Notice that we are not comparing the strength of our inner resources and the strength of our outer challenge directly. Rather, we are comparing our *perception* of our inner strength with our *perception* of our outer challenge. This makes a huge difference, because our perception is our reality. And we act more frequently out of our perception than we do out of the actual reality.

Our perception of our inner resources is, of course, inside us. But so is our perception of our outer challenge inside us. We hold an image of our challenge in our mind, making it bigger or smaller, overwhelming and intimidating, or challenging and beatable.

Think of our attitudes as having two competing perceptions inside us: (1) our attitude about the strength of our inner resources and (2) our attitude about the strength of our outer challenge. Our challenge, for all practical purposes, is inside us. This is not to deny that the mountain is there — it is only to say that whether we climb that mountain or not is related more to the content of our attitude, about ourself and the mountain, than it is to the mountain itself. The mountain has a range, so to speak, of becoming bigger or smaller in our mind, based upon our inner attitude toward it. And we have a range of becoming bigger or smaller based upon our attitude about our own inner strength.

Approaching life from this vantage point will produce better results, more happiness, more success and more of a feeling of being in control of your destiny. When you accept the struggle as inside, it's within you to manage the relative strength of both you and your challenge. The mountain becomes more manageable. You become the manager.

New Attitude Nutrients offer you two ways to grow: (1) increase the strength of your attitude toward your own inner resources and/or (2) decrease your perception of the strength of your challenge.

NUTRITIONAL ANALYSIS OF NEW ATTITUDE NUTRIENTS

New Attitude Nutrients are designed to strengthen our thoughts, feelings and actions, to maximize our inner resources in an effort to accurately perceive, and then to exceed, our inner and outer challenge.

New Attitude Nutrients then strengthen our thoughts, feelings and actions. Why are our attitudes so important in our life? What are the benefits of strengthening our attitudes? Can our attitudes, like our bodies, even be strengthened with nutrients?

Let's take a few minutes to understand the importance of our attitudes.

WE ARE OUR ATTITUDES

Physically speaking, we are our bodies. Socially speaking, we are ourselves in relation to others. Spiritually speaking, we are ourselves in relation to something deeper and more permanent than our "self."

And psychologically speaking, we are our attitudes! The important influence of our attitudes in life has been known for a long time.

Researching the historical background on attitude, we find that over 2,000 years ago, the stoic philosopher Epictetus concluded that humans are not disturbed by the things that happen to them, but rather *humans are disturbed by the inner attitude they take toward these outside factors*.

Some sixteen centuries later, another philosopher, Baruch Spinoza, asserted that for as long as we believe that some dream is impossible, for that exact period of time it will be impossible. But the very moment we determine that the achievement is possible is the moment we move toward conquering that challenge in our life. In other words, when facing seemingly insurmountable odds in our outside world, our attitude will determine whether we go forward or become frustrated and retreat. And that something inside us, our attitude, is something that we personally determine. We are our attitudes!

Two hundred years later, philosopher Immanuel Kant observed that *the way we perceive our experiences has more of an impact on us than do our actual experiences*. Is it possible that we are more affected by the attitudes we choose to take toward our world than we are by our actual worldly experiences? If so, are our attitudes more consequential to our happiness and success in life than our actual experiences? After all, we don't always choose our experiences, but, as you will see, we do choose our attitudes. We are our attitudes!

We can prove that our attitude is more influential than the "outside" experience. Have you ever been part of a group of people who experienced the same "outside" setback, perhaps a delayed flight, a failed test or a devastating tornado? Did every person have the same reaction? Of course not. Some were devastated, but some found strength.

Same event outside. Different attitude inside. With New Attitude Nutrients, we are not the helpless victims of our outside environment. With attitude nutrients, we realize that we are the creators of our actions and reactions in life. When we strengthen our attitudes, we strengthen the very core of us. Because we are our attitudes!

OUR ATTITUDE CHOICES ARE LIMITLESS

After almost a hundred years of observing life, nineteenth century philosopher Bertrand Russell commented on the unlimited human possibilities by concluding that, "In the vast realm of the alive, creative human mind, there are no limitations."

In 1927, optimistic psychiatrist Alfred Adler argued that humans were dramatically different from other animals in at least one way. Adler believed that humans could dream, create, decide, choose and invent many attitudes they took toward their lives. They were unlimited in their choices. Adler wrote to his pupil Heinz Ansbacher:

> *Do not forget the most important fact that not heredity, and not environment, are determining factors. Both are giving only the frame and influences which are answered by the individual in regard to his styled creative power.*

Even the forces of heredity and environment are not ultimate determiners. That's why *no psychological study ever conducted showed a perfect relationship between outside conditions and inside attitude.*

We are our attitudes. Our attitude choices are limitless. We are limitless!

Psychiatrist Victor Frankl wrote about his experiences in a prisoner-of-war camp with little chance of survival. Frankl said that the guards could do anything they wanted to him — starve him, stone him, freeze him, attempt to dehumanize him. Then Frankl experienced a reawakening of his inner attitude toward his outer challenge by concluding that although the guards could do anything they wanted to him, *the one thing the guards couldn't do was affect the way he chose to view his life.* That private vital source of strength was something inside of him, his attitude, and out of the reach of any external force. His nutrients kept him going, even in the absence of food, water and other nourishment.

Another philosopher, William James, enlarged our realization of our potential by exalting that, "*Only humans have the ability to change their outer world, by first changing their inner world.*" Our attitude choices our limitless. We are not victims; we are creators!

NEW ATTITUDE NUTRIENTS AND SELF-ACTUALIZATION

Some of the early beliefs about the capabilities of human beings were based on Sigmund Freud's couch sample of emotionally disturbed, hurting, unhappy, self-defeating individuals. No wonder Freud's bleak conclusions about the human possibility! But Freud's dwelling on the attitude of helplessness does not apply to you today. My guess is that Freud never met *you*! He probably never saw a patient like you, and it was from his patients that he drew his conclusions. Sure your unconscious mind influences some of your motivations, but so does your conscious and subconscious mind as well. Did your ever *consciously* set a goal, *consciously* follow your plan and *consciously* celebrate as you reached your goal?

About the same time young Albert Ellis was formulating his unique ideas, Abraham Maslow decided to study a healthier sample of people than Freud's. Maslow sought out, found and studied the attitudes of the healthiest, happiest humans. The curious psychologist observed from his sample that change was possible, at any age. Maslow shifted the thinking of a society which was still looking down from Freud's pessimism and obsessing with, "What's wrong here? How is this person diseased and limited?" to look up and begin a new day by sensing, "What's right here? What are this person's assets, strengths, resources and, most importantly, potential?" Maslow started a cultural and professional revolution by transforming our human condition paradigm from the "disease model" to the "wellness or potential model"! The human potential movement was beginning.

In *The Farther Reaches of Human Nature* (1954), Maslow wrote:

> *On the whole I think it is fair to say that human history is a record of the ways in which human nature has been sold short. The highest possibilities of human nature have practically always been underrated. Even when good specimens — the saints, the sages, and the great leaders of history — have been studied, the temptation too often has been to consider them not human, but supernaturally endowed.*

Maslow referred to the attitudes he found present in the healthiest, happiest, most fulfilled humans as "self-actualizing." Self-actualizing means that these individuals actualized, or made real, more of their human potential. Like the seed that becomes the giant oak, self-actualizing individuals reached higher to express more of their possibilities. Their attitudes enabled them to transcend those environmental ceilings placed in the way of their will.

Maslow found the following attitudes present in the thoughts, feelings and behaviors of self-actualizing people. Notice the appropriate New Attitude Nutrient that develops each particular attitude. You will be acquiring the seeds of self-actualization throughout the next seven chapters in *TODAY!*

1. *Self-actualizing people have a clearer perception of reality and a more comfortable relationship with reality* (New Attitude Nutrient #3: ACCEPTANCE)

2. *Self-actualizing people are more spontaneous and experience each moment as an end in itself, not as a means to another end* (New Attitude Nutrient #6: INSPIRATION)

3. *Self-actualizing people have a greater desire for private time to regenerate strength, undiluted by environmental drains on their thinking, feeling and behavior* (New Attitude Nutrient #2: INNER SECURITY)

4. *Self-actualizing people have a social interest in community and humanity. They experience themselves as proactively being the momentum makers to shape a better world* (New Attitude Nutrient #7: LEADERSHIP)

5. *The self-actualizing person is problem or challenge centered, not ego centered* (New Attitude Nutrient #6: INSPIRATION)

6. *The self-actualizing person is autonomous, independent of culture and environment* (New Attitude Nutrient #2: INNER SECURITY)

7. *The self-actualizing person has deeper and more meaningful interpersonal relationships* (New Attitude Nutrient #4: UNDERSTANDING)

8. *The self-actualizing person has an expanded viewpoint* (New Attitude Nutrient #1: PURPOSE & PASSION)

9. *The self-actualizing person accepts self and others* (New Attitude Nutrient #4: UNDERSTANDING)

10. *The self-actualizing person has a democratic character structure* (New Attitude Nutrient #7: LEADERSHIP)

11. *The self-actualizing person has a continued freshness of appreciation* (New Attitude Nutrient #1: PURPOSE & PASSION)

12. *The self-actualizing person is more creative* (New Attitude Nutrient #5: COURAGE)

By acquiring these New Attitude Nutrients, you will find yourself moving in the direction of self-actualization, not almost immediately but immediately. Now! *TODAY!*

THE MOMENT OF BIRTH OF NEW ATTITUDE NUTRIENTS

When the ideas throughout history from Epictetus to Kant, Russell, Adler, James, Frankl and Maslow were brought to the psychotherapeutic clinic of Albert Ellis, the whole helpless side of the psychological community one day lost its reason to wring its hopeless, sweaty hands. Albert Ellis raised some questions in the mid-fifties that loosened the imaginary steel grip that heredity and environment held on humankind. Our minds, hearts and bodies were freed!

Let's put all of Ellis's questions into one:

> *If one thousand people all experienced the same outside, external event, would all one thousand people have exactly the same resultant inside reaction in response to the same outside stimulus?*

Of course not! Aren't there a number of possible perceptual, emotive and behavioral alternatives that might be chosen by the person whose mind, heart and body are creating a response to the outside situation? If there are any limits, they would be in the unwilling stretch of one's mind, heart and body.

Couldn't there be a variety of chosen responses to such experiences as being turned down for a job, failing a test, experiencing a rejection, losing a contract or an important game, or even losing a friend?

Some individuals, at one end of the reaction range, would be devastated for a long time. Others, in the middle, would be upset for a while, and perhaps eventually bounce back. And still others, at the upper range of possible reactions to the same event, would find some nutrients for growth in the same event. Some would choose to create a comeback attitude. They would be the ones with purpose and passion, inner security, acceptance, understanding, courage, inspiration and leadership skills.

Ellis's question proved Epictetus's observation from two millennia earlier. It's not what happens to us in life that affects us but rather the view we take of it. The fact that different people respond differently to the same external event proves that a person's attitude is a better determinant of that person's future than is the person's actual experience.

And so psychology became one of the nutritional sciences. We now have New Attitude Nutrients, or nutrients to grow our thoughts, feelings and actions.

Epictetus, Spinoza, Kant, Adler, James, Frankl, Maslow and Ellis's rational emotive behavior therapy are responsible for one of the most powerful breakthroughs of the twenty-first century.

OUR CRISES OFFER THE MOST MEANINGFUL NUTRIENTS

New Attitude Nutrients strengthen us regardless of environmental events, positive or negative. As one anonymous source proclaimed, "Anything that doesn't kill me only makes me stronger." Attitude nutrients give us strength, no matter what.

For example, suppose our attitude is that we are going to gain knowledge and insight from every life experience, without judging it as good or bad. The fact is, we probably gain more insight from an experience most people call bad than we do from a good one. Could just having that attitude help us see that crises and tough experiences give us information that we would not have had without the setback? Through the right attitude, could hardship actually give us strength? With the wrong attitude, could the same hardship actually weaken us? That is the power of attitudinal nutrients!

Think about a difficult experience in your past. What did you learn from the experience that is still with you today, making you stronger for your future? Is it possible that you believe you can handle more today because of what you showed yourself you could handle then?

By mastering the next few sections on attitudes, you will hold the master key to understanding New Attitude Nutrients.

ATTITUDES ARE MORE THAN JUST BELIEFS

It is easy to confuse an attitude with a thought or a belief or an overall view. In actuality, however, our attitudes are much broader than our thoughts or beliefs. Attitudes have three components. Our attitudes are composed of (1) our thinking, our beliefs and our viewpoint; (2) our feelings or emotions and (3) our actions or behaviors.

$$Attitudes = Thoughts + Feelings + Actions$$

Attitudes, or our thoughts, feelings and actions, have been documented to dramatically influence our emotional and physical health, happiness, well-being, even our longevity, our success or failure in life, as well as the quality of our relationships. Our attitudes are linked not only with our general intelligence, but with the more recently discovered concepts of *emotional intelligence* by Daniel Goleman and *successful intelligence* by Robert J. Sternberg.

If we could develop only one aspect of ourselves, it strikes me that our best choice would be our attitudes.

Would you rather have many things in life but a poor attitude, or would you rather have very little in life but a great attitude? You have probably met people in both circumstances. Who did you respect more? If you have the right attitude, you can successfully accumulate those things that represent success for you.

To better understand New Attitude Nutrients, let's compare them to two popular forms of success and self-help: positive thinking and behavior modification.

NEW ATTITUDE NUTRIENTS:
3 × THE POWER OF POSITIVE THINKING

Positive thinking continues to make a huge contribution to helping people become healthier, happier and even wealthier in life. Positive thinking is similar to New Attitude Nutrients in that both provide positive, growth-promoting nourishment through thought modification. After encouraging positive thinking with their patients, many psychologists noticed that although it often worked, sometimes it didn't.

Positive thinking works for those people whose Dominant Attitude Style is thinking — as opposed to the other two components of attitude, that is, feeling and acting. (You will soon discover your Dominant Attitude Style. This will provide you with an important tool for awareness of both self and others.) A person whose Dominant Attitude Style is thinking is able to use positive thinking techniques, which often result in changes in the other two components of attitude: feeling and acting. Success!

However, for a person whose Dominant Attitude Style is feeling, positive thinking often flops. Let's consider an example. Have you ever encouraged somebody to *think* differently about a situation, and they changed their thoughts but still felt the same? Thinking changes didn't change feelings, except maybe the person felt a little annoyed, accusing your well-intentioned suggestion of being insensitive.

Let's look at another example. Maybe you know at a thinking or belief level that it would be the right thing to do to tell your father you love him or to forgive a friend for something he or she did to you years ago. You even feel guilty at a feeling level. You know what you should do and you feel you should do it, but you just can't act on it. You can't get yourself to *do*, to change one component of your attitude, your actions. That's because positive thinking covers one-third of an attitude, a person's thoughts.

POSITIVE THINKING CHANGES THOUGHTS: NEW ATTITUDE NUTRIENTS CHANGE ATTITUDES

Positive thinking is a part of New Attitude Nutrients. While positive thinking focuses on changing thoughts, New Attitude Nutrients change total attitudes, that is, (1) thinking, (2) feeling and (3) acting or doing. Positive thinking is effective when a person's thoughts successfully change the way the person feels and acts in life. Positive thinking is ineffective when all the person changes is his or her thoughts, and there is no other attitudinal change.

Review

Try to summarize for yourself the difference between positive thinking and New Attitude Nutrients.

What are the three components of an attitude?

Why might it be suggested that New Attitude Nutrients are three times the power of positive thinking?

Now let's do one more brief comparison. This time we'll consider the difference between New Attitude Nutrients and another system of personal growth, behavior modification.

SUPPLEMENTS FOR YOUR BEHAVIOR MODIFICATION EXERCISE, WEIGHT LOSS OR PARENTING PROGRAM

Positive thinking changes thoughts, one-third of total attitude change. Behavior modification is an approach that focuses on changing our actions or behaviors, another component of attitude. If we condition and reinforce ourselves, through behavior modification, to change our nail-biting behavior during final exams, and we experience our anxious thoughts and feelings also changing, then we have made a total attitude change. If, however, only our behavior changes, we have not made a total attitude change.

Behavior modification tends to work if a person's Dominant Attitude Style is acting or doing. Behavior modification is successful when the total attitude of a person is changed. And behavior modification is unsuccessful when only the behaviors, and not the thoughts or feelings, are changed.

New Attitude Nutrients focus on the total attitude change because partial change offers only a one-third chance of success. New Attitude Nutrients agree with the behavioral school in those instances where a person has an acting–doing Dominant Attitude Style.

Suppose you are using behavior modification to condition yourself to exercise for one hour a day. You keep charts and reward yourself with tokens or stars that represent working toward your goal. If your program is effective, and keeps you going and going, your behavior modification is effective.

If, however, you start off strong and then lose interest, chances are you need to engage the other two components of your Dominant Attitude Style — your thinking and your feeling. Changing your thinking might involve creating a list of a dozen logical positive reasons to show why it would be advantageous for you to go forward. Follow that up by creating a list of logical negative consequences if you were to stop. Can you see how this would be effective for a Think-er?

You may also need support for your change by engaging your feelings. Here you might post a long list of affirmations or positive thoughts to keep you going. You might also use your emotions, if you are a Feel-er, to be the fuel to fire yourself up to get started. (This won't work too well if you are a Think-er or Do-er, or an action person. It might be too "shallow" for you to use affirmations, since they may seem like obsessions that aren't really necessary.)

You might think of how you could use New Attitude Nutrients to supplement your weight loss program as well. If you are a Think-er, you would make an overpowering list of all of the logical benefits of losing weight and an even more overpowering list of all of the negative consequences of losing weight. If you are a Feel-er, you would generate inner excitement about how each substitution of a more nutritious, less fattening food is moving you closer to your ideal physical state. And if you are a Do-er, you would take action, now, to get the job done.

Building long-term responsibility in a child involves developing an intrinsically (driven from within) motivated child. This is opposed to building an extrinsically motivated child, who needs to be pushed by you, every day! Think of the consequences of a parent praising a child. If the parent says, "I like what you are doing. Good job!" the child is being reinforced for doing something that someone older, bigger and stronger approves of. The child becomes extrinsically motivated, doing something because of being driven by an outside force. When the outside force — the parent — isn't around, the child has no reason to act a certain way, because the motivation isn't inside — it's outside!

A more effective approach is to involve New Attitude Nutrients and encouragement by building the child *to personally want to* perform because of inner-driven thoughts, feelings and actions. Don Dinkmeyer and I discussed the contrast between praise and encouragement in *The Skills of Encouragement*.

Consider how encouragement differs from praise:

> *Praise: "I like what you did. It's great!"*
>
> *Encouragement: How do you FEEL about your work? It sure seems like you enjoy drawing! What do you THINK about it? Do you think you like the colors you chose? What goal do you have of DOING next?"*

With encouragement, the child starts pushing himself or herself from within, and slowly moves away from the need to be constantly praised, punished, pushed and pulled by others. (You will learn much more about intrinsic motivation in the chapter on Inner Security Nutrients.)

Remember: Behavior modification changes behaviors; New Attitude Nutrients change attitudes. Unless there is a total change in thoughts, feelings and actions, there would not be enough supplements to keep the new attitude intact. That is why a total approach is not only more effective, but relatively more permanent.

Now, lets consider the seven growth directions you will be experiencing through the use of New Attitude Nutrients.

DIRECTIONS OF PERSONAL GROWTH WITH NEW ATTITUDE NUTRIENTS

These are seven major attitude directions (thoughts, feelings and actions) that New Attitude Nutrients focus on growing in you:

Growth-Inhibiting Attitudes	*Growth-Promoting Attitudes*
Moving from...	**Growing...**
1. Aimlessness	1. Passion with a purpose
2. Environmental dependency	2. Inner security
3. Frustration	3. Acceptance
4. Judging others	4. Understanding others
5. Fears and anxieties	5. Courage
6. Ego-centered	6. Spirited energy
7. Follower	7. Leader

ANALYZING YOUR DOMINANT ATTITUDE STYLE

In order for you to determine the most effective way of acquiring your New Attitude Nutrients, it is vital to determine your Dominant Attitude Style. Take a few moments to answer the questions below. Put a number 3 in front of the phrase that is most true of you, a 2 in front of the one that is next true of you and a 1 in front of the statement that is least true of you. In close calls, try your best. Answer each question with a 3, a 2 and a 1.

1. What is my first reaction when facing a project to be done?
    A. ____ I swing into action, get into it and get it done
    B. ____ I start thinking and planning my approach
    C. ____ I feel something inside me about the project
2. When am I most happy?
    A. ____ When I am active and moving
    B. ____ When I am aware of my feelings
    C. ____ When I am thinking about or planning something
3. What have most of my decisions in life been based upon?
    A. ____ My gut reactions
    B. ____ My desire to get moving
    C. ____ What makes sense
4. Where should I be placed on our team to best use me?
    A. ____ The role of understanding others' feelings
    B. ____ The planner for the future
    C. ____ The work force to make things happen

5. If people have a flaw, what do I think it most frequently is?
    A. ___ Too much thinking, not enough doing
    B. ___ Taking action without planning ahead
    C. ___ Not putting their hearts into what they are doing

6. When am I most tense?
    A. ___ When the future looks uncertain
    B. ___ When I don't have anything to do
    C. ___ When I'm not sure how I am feeling

7. What is the best way for someone to motivate me?
    A. ___ If they give me reasons why the job is important
    B. ___ If they take some time to first understand my feelings
    C. ___ If they tell me what to do and let me loose

8. What kind of a leader do I like best?
    A. ___ One who tells me what to do
    B. ___ One who wants me to plan for the best approach
    C. ___ One who understands my feelings

9. What do people tend to think my biggest problem is?
    A. ___ I don't look before I leap
    B. ___ I look too long before I leap
    C. ___ I'm too concerned about feelings

10. What is the most frequent reason why I don't get something done?
    A. ___ I just didn't follow through
    B. ___ I just wasn't feeling inspired
    C. ___ I just didn't think it was important enough

Now transfer your responses from your Dominant Attitude Style survey to the chart below. Notice that the order of the letters may change for each question.

1.	B. ___	C. ___	A. ___
2.	C. ___	B. ___	A. ___
3.	C. ___	A. ___	B. ___
4.	B. ___	A. ___	C. ___
5.	C. ___	A. ___	B. ___
6.	A. ___	C. ___	B. ___
7.	A. ___	B. ___	C. ___
8.	B. ___	C. ___	A. ___
9.	B. ___	C. ___	A. ___
10.	C. ___	B. ___	A. ___
TOTAL	___	___	___

Total of 3 columns equals 60

What Is Your Dominant Attitude Style?

Higher scores in the first column suggest **you are moved or motivated first by thinking (Think-er).**

Higher scores in the second column suggest **you are moved or motivated first by feelings (Feel-er).**

Higher scores in the third column suggest **you are moved or motivated by action or doing (Do-er).**

The average score is 20. A score of 22 or 23 demonstrates a tendency toward that Dominant Attitude Style, whereas a score of 24 or above indicates a strong dominant style. A balance among the three attitude components is demonstrated when all three scores hover around 19–20–21. The lowest score indicates your recessive area.

Before listing your highest to lowest scores in order to determine your approach to acquiring your New Attitude Nutrients, note the seven possible arrangements of Dominant Attitude Style, one of which is similar to yours:

1. Think-er/Feel-er/Do-er
2. Think-er/Do-er/Feel-er
3. Feel-er/Think-er/Do-er
4. Feel-er/Do-er/Think-er
5. Do-er/Think-er/Feel-er
6. Do-er/Feel-er/Think-er
7. No dominant attitude preference, balanced style of
    19 to 21 each

List the arrangement of your Dominant Attitude Style from highest to lowest:

_____   _____   _____

This will determine the order in which you will be acquiring your New Attitude Nutrients. First, let's explore the meaning and characteristics of each attitude style.

CHARACTERISTICS OF EACH DOMINANT ATTITUDE STYLE

Think-er

1. A Think-er is moved primarily by thoughts, logic, reasoning and what makes sense. A Think-er uses mental charts of the advantages and disadvantages of taking certain courses of action.
2. A Think-er loves planning ahead.
3. A Think-er likes a reasonable amount of certainty before moving ahead.
4. A Think-er moves based on solid facts.
5. A Think-er handles anxiety or uncertainty by planning to the last detail to make sure all variables are controlled before proceeding.
6. A Think-er tends to view a Feel-er as soft, too subjective, too emotional and not logical enough.
7. Think-ers tend to view Do-ers as restless and moving, too impulsive and sure to get burned if they don't slow down.
8. Without Think-ers, the world would have less reason, planning, logic and structure. Everyone would be worse off.
9. If you are a Think-er, you will be acquiring your New Attitude Nutrients through the thinking exercises first, and then immersing yourself in your second most dominant style next.

Feel-er

1. A Feel-er is moved or motivated primarily by feelings and emotions. Something inside the Feel-er is very important, more important in getting the Feel-er moving than facts. Feelings are more important than facts.

2. A Feel-er is more spontaneous than a Think-er, because a Feel-er's sense of certainty comes from those emotions he or she is experiencing now. A Feel-er is more in tune with himself or herself on a moment-to-moment basis. When guided by feelings, a Feel-er doesn't plan ahead, as does the Think-er.

3. A Feel-er handles anxiety or uncertainty by getting into it. This reaction toward anxiety confuses the Think-er, who is trying to think of a plan to avoid anxiety. A Feel-er lets anxiety in, which is stressful to a Do-er, who is running away, demanding the Feel-er "do something about it."

4. A Feel-er tends to experience Think-ers as cold and boring.

5. A Feel-er tends to experience Do-ers as keeping active to avoid getting in touch with themselves.

6. Without Feel-ers, the world would have less passion and poetry, less joy and perhaps less love.

7. If you are a Feel-er, you will start acquiring your New Attitude Nutrients by feeling the feeling exercises first and then moving to the second of your dominant styles.

Do-er

1. A Do-er is moved or motivated by physically or mentally getting something done, moving from here to there. A Do-er gets right into it, gets his or her hands dirty and keeps moving. Do-ers like to see results — progress.

2. A Do-er can be seen at a party dangling his or her car keys, ready to go, while the Feel-er is talking, opening up or listening to someone, and the Think-er is sitting on the couch planning the next day.

3. A Do-er expresses himself or herself with movements and gestures and can't sit still. A Do-er handles anxiety by kind of shaking it off.

4. A Do-er wants to make something happen and gets frustrated with Feel-ers, because feeling isn't doing something.

5. A Do-er tends to experience a Think-er as afraid to act and move. Do-ers wonder what Thinkers are doing when they are thinking. The only thing that counts to the Do-er is results.

6. Without Do-ers, a lot less would be accomplished and there would be little follow-through. Do-ers make things happen!

7. If Do-er is your Dominant Attitude Style, start doing the Do-er exercises first; then move on to your second and third dominant styles, in that order.

USING NEW ATTITUDE NUTRIENTS WITH YOUR DOMINANT ATTITUDE STYLE

In the preceding pages, you learned your Dominant Attitude Style.

For each of the 7 New Attitude Nutrients, after a brief description of the nutrient and why it is important, a series of New Attitude Nutrient acquisition exercises is provided. They will look like this:

THINK

1.
2.
3.

FEEL

1.
2.
3.

DO

1.
2.
3.

Do the exercises in order of arrangement of your Dominant Attitude Style. A Feel-er/Think-er/Do-er would start with the feeling exercises, and then proceed to thinking and doing. You will most effectively grow through these seven attitude nutrients by starting with your Dominant Attitude Style until it is acquired, then moving to your second until it is experienced, and then moving on to your third or most recessive style until that style is transformed. You are ready. Your task is vital. Plan on winning!

THE 7 NEW
ATTITUDE NUTRIENTS

#1 PURPOSE & PASSION Nutrient:
"I know where I'm going, and I'm going to get there!"

#2 INNER SECURITY Nutrient:
"I have every resource inside me to get me to my dreams, even without any environmental support."

#3 ACCEPTANCE Nutrient:
"What is, is!"

#4 UNDERSTANDING Nutrient:
"The surest way toward rewarding relationships is to understand others to help them get what they need."

#5 COURAGE Nutrient:
"I have the courage to flow through my anxieties to enter my New Attitude Growth Zone!"

#6 INSPIRATION Nutrient:
"My spirit is stronger than my ego."

#7 LEADERSHIP Nutrient:
"One person with a dream can change the world."

New Attitude Nutrient #1

℞: PURPOSE & PASSION NUTRIENT

"Today, I'll determine where I will be tomorrow!"

"Have you ever noticed that the only ones who reach their dreams... are those who have them?"

Measuring the effectiveness of the PURPOSE & PASSION Nutrient for your life

✔ Nutrient to find meaning and create dreams, goals, success (Thought)

✔ Nutrient for enthusiasm, high spirits, desire for achievement (Feeling)

✔ Nutrient to take action and reach dreams (Action)

You'll sense the effectiveness of the PURPOSE & PASSION Nutrient in the moments when you experience you have something that is important to do in your life and you are determined to do it.

PURPOSE & PASSION Nutrients are produced to inhibit or protect you against the development of the following common symptoms:

- ✔ aimlessness
- ✔ apathy
- ✔ confusion
- ✔ hopelessness
- ✔ lack of meaning and purpose in life
- ✔ loss of passion
- ✔ mid-life crisis
- ✔ needing direction
- ✔ some forms of depression

When used as recommended, you can expect growth in the following areas from PURPOSE & PASSION Nutrients:

- ✔ deeper purpose in life
- ✔ development of a purposeful plan
- ✔ enthusiasm
- ✔ heightened passion
- ✔ motivation
- ✔ new goals
- ✔ renewal

How to Get the Best Advice in Your World

Where were you ten years ago? What insights and feelings do you have today that you didn't have then? Imagine if you could talk to your younger self now. What is the single most important piece of advice that you could offer to your younger self based upon what you have learned in the last decade?

Now let's imagine that ten years from now you are speaking to yourself today. What do you believe will be the single most important thing you would tell yourself to do today? Now. While you can! What will you wish ten years from now that you would do today? Close your book and take a few minutes to really get into listening to yourself.

Continuing, let's create an imaginary comparison and discussion between your present you and your future you, ten years from now.

✔ Which one seems wiser?
✔ Which one thinks bigger?
✔ Which one has a greater purpose?
✔ Which one has more belief?
✔ Which one is building you up and which one is tearing you down?
✔ Which one has more doubts?
✔ Which one's attitude would you like to have?

Suppose the two of you, your present you and your future you, were talking to each other. Take a few minutes and imagine how the conversation might go.

- ✔ Start by having your present you tell your future you about a current challenge, problem, conflict, crisis or struggle you are facing today.
- ✔ Next have your future you share with your present you some thoughts, feelings and suggested actions based upon advance experience and expanded perspective.

Close your book again, and talk with your wise older self, seeking wisdom from within.

Now have your future you identify three actions to take today that are important for you in the long range:

1.

2.

3.

Now decide, from your future you vantage point, which one of the three is most crucial. Check that one off. You have now established at least one great starting point.

Importance of the PURPOSE & PASSION New Attitude Nutrient

Have you ever noticed that the only ones who reach their dreams are those who have them? Why is that? Without a dream, there is no purpose, no pull or push. With no point to aim at, life is pointless and aimless. Without a destination, you can't take charge of your destiny.

Imagine the Super Bowl played without any goal lines. Where do you run? It really doesn't matter where you run, does it? It doesn't even matter if you show up! Imagine being in an airplane when the pilot suggests he doesn't know where he is going. When we have no goal or purpose, we are playing without a goal line. We are directionless in life.

Determining your destination determines your destiny. Taking a PURPOSE & PASSION Nutrient gives you at least three advantages over wandering aimlessly:

1. A goal gives you a purpose, and you are immediately consciously and even subconsciously lifted. Even in your sleep, your mind and heart will be finding ways to reach your goal or dream. (Thinking)
2. A goal gives you not only a purpose, but passion. Passion ignites your enthusiasm, which is your energy to transform your creative ideas and thought into life-changing actions. (Feeling)
3. A firmly locked-in goal shows you the direction to move in. When you are lost or confused, a goal shows you where you are in relation to it. And gets you moving again. (Action)

Without a purpose and without passion, you lose these three attitudinal advantages. Plus, you lose the satisfaction of achieving something that is very important to you. How much does it cost you not to have a purpose in life?

PURPOSE & PASSION New Attitude Nutrient — Acquisition Exercises

Remember to proceed by acquiring your New Attitude Nutrients in the order of arrangement of your Dominant Attitude Style, from 1 to 3.

THINK

Think-ers start here, Feel-ers start at FEEL and Do-ers start at the DO exercises. Then proceed to your second strongest Dominant Attitude Style, etc.

1. What do you think is the most important goal in your life?
    ✔ How will you know when your goal is reached?
    ✔ By what date will you reach your goal?
    ✔ Plan the first five steps to take to reach your goal:

    1.

    2.

    3.

4.

5.

2. What negative habit do you think you would like to stop, beginning today?
   ✔ Think of four powerful logical reasons to stop this habit now.

   1.

   2.

   3.

   4.

   ✔ Think of three logical reasons why your life will be better five years from now if you stop your habit now.

   1.

   2.

   3.

3. List some one-year goals for yourself in the following five areas of your life:
   ✔ Physical goals (appearance, ideal weight, etc.)

✔ Social self (social qualities you are going to develop)
✔ Professional self
✔ Financial self
✔ Spiritual self

4. How do you think you would like to make your workplace, your community and your world a better place?
    ✔ Workplace
    ✔ Community
    ✔ World

5. Make a list of one hundred experiences or achievements you would like to accomplish during your lifetime. Each one can be as small as trying a new food or as big as climbing Mt. Everest. If you make this list, a week later you will have checked off at least ten items. If you don't make this list, in the same period of time you will have checked off none. Thinking this through will get you better results than not doing it.

    1.

    2.

    3.

    4.

    5.

    6.

7.

8.

9.

10.

11.

12.

13.

14.

15.

16.

17.

18.

19.

20.

21.

22.

23.

24.

25.

26.

27.

28.

29.

30.

31.

32.

33.

34.

35.

36.

37.

38.

39.

40.

41.

42.

43.

44.

45.

46.

47.

48.

49.

50.

51.

52.

53.

54.

55.

56.

57.

58.

59.

60.

61.

62.

63.

64.

65.

66.

67.

68.

69.

70.

71.

72.

73.

74.

75.

76.

77.

78.

79.

80.

81.

82.

83.

84.

85.

86.

87.

88.

89.

90.

91.

92.

93.

94.

95.

96.

97.

98.

99.

100.

Remember to check off each one as you experience or achieve it. You might want to write down the date as well.

<u>FEEL</u> (FEEL-ERS START HERE)

1. Get right into your guts. What dream do you have
    a burning passion, a fire inside you, to accomplish?
    What do you want more than anything else in your
    life? Let your heart speak to you about how impor-
    tant this mission is for you and your life. (Take a
    few minutes to feel your role in accomplishing
    something very important to you.)
    ✔ List your passionate desire for achievement here:

    ✔ How will you feel as you get started in reaching
      this dream?
    ✔ How will you feel when you are in the process
      of reaching this dream?
    ✔ How will you feel when your reach your dream?
    ✔ When will you reach your important dream?

2. What *cause* generates passion in you and creates a
    deep feeling inside that you want to commit yourself
    to it?
    ✔ How will you feel as you get started?
    ✔ How will you feel when you are in the process
      of helping?
    ✔ How will you feel when you find that you
      changed the world?
    ✔ Is it worth those feelings?

3. Fire up your feelings, your passion to keep your
    thinking part really thinking to find ways and your
    acting part taking action to reach your purpose in
    life. If you have a weak area, which one would it

be: thinking, feeling or acting? From which other area can you gain additional strength?

✔ Always remember to mobilize the other two components of your attitudinal resources to overcompensate for the recessive area. Recall that the primary reason we don't reach our dreams is because our weakest area of thinking, feeling and doing holds us back. We are only as strong as our weakest attitudinal link.

<u>DO</u> (DO-ERS START HERE)

The only thing that ultimately matters is making things happen, getting things done. What purpose can you get yourself moving toward today? How much is possible in only one day? One year? Ten years? A lifetime?

✔ Take action. What will you immediately start to accomplish today?

✔ What will your first step be?

✔ When will you know that you are finished?

✔ What strength will you need from your Think-er?

✔ What help will you need from your Feel-er?

You can tell if the New Attitude Nutrients are working. Do you now have a purpose, a direction, a goal, a dream?

✔ What is your deeper purpose?

✔ What are your three major thoughts and plans?

    1.

    2.

    3.

✔ What feelings inside you will provide energy to your thoughts and actions to keep you going?

    1.

    2.

    3.

✔ What actions are you going to take today?

    1.

    2.

    3.

PURPOSE & PASSION New Attitude Nutrient — Acquisition Check

Our goal at the beginning of this chapter was to achieve three changes in your attitude: a change in thoughts, a change in feelings and a change in actions.

You can measure the effectiveness of the PURPOSE & PASSION Nutrient by asking yourself three questions:

- ✔ Have I found more meaning in life, created a new dream or set some new goals for myself? (Thought)
- ✔ Am I more enthusiastic, are my spirits increased and do I have a greater desire for achievement? (Feeling)
- ✔ Am I taking action now to reach my new dreams? (Action)

Get started. With a purpose outside and a passion inside.

R: INNER SECURITY NUTRIENT

"Today, I'll build my inner resources to rise above the outer forces!"

"Waiting for my world to change before I change is like looking into the mirror at my reflection and saying, 'You move first, then I'll move.' There is a better way. When I move, my reflection moves. Every time!"

Measuring the effectiveness of the INNER SECURITY Nutrient for your life

✔ Nutrient to affirm inner assets, strengths and resources to succeed (Thought)
✔ Nutrient for security, self-confidence, self-reliance, inner knowing (Feeling)
✔ Nutrient to take self-determined action, without outside support (Action)

You'll sense the effectiveness of the INNER SECURITY Nutrient in those moments when you find that your own inner knowing is as vital to you as outer approval is.

INNER SECURITY Nutrients are produced to inhibit or protect against the development of the following common symptoms:

- ✔ need for approval from others
- ✔ blaming, excusing
- ✔ co-dependency
- ✔ dependency
- ✔ dwelling on what's wrong with yourself
- ✔ feeling of rejection
- ✔ focusing on mistakes
- ✔ jealousy
- ✔ loss of confidence
- ✔ self-doubt

When used as recommended, you can expect growth in the following areas from INNER SECURITY Nutrients:

- ✔ centering on your assets, strengths and resources
- ✔ focusing on what's right with you
- ✔ inner strength
- ✔ intrinsic motivation
- ✔ personal responsibility
- ✔ self-confidence
- ✔ self-determination
- ✔ self-encouragement
- ✔ trust in yourself

TRUST YOURSELF

- ✔ At twenty, we are devastated when others are talking about us.
- ✔ At forty, we find that we can finally deal with others talking about us.
- ✔ At sixty, we realize they were never talking about us in the first place!

What would you do if, from this moment on, for the rest of your life, no one anywhere ever again approved of your actions, applauded you or ever acknowledged you or said, "great job"?

Would you still survive? Would you go crazy for approval? Would you doubt yourself endlessly? Would you be weaker and less secure ten years from now?

Or would you start gaining strength from within to keep going forward, driven by your own inner knowing? Would you start realizing that others are probably also so busy being caught up in waiting for approval from others that they don't have any time to approve of you? Wouldn't it be vital and important to acquire the INNER SECURITY Nutrient to build your own inner strength to go forward, even without environmental support and approval?

Importance of the INNER SECURITY New Attitude Nutrient

Is your security foundation outside or inside of you?

We need to get our foundation of support and motivation from some source. And that source can be in our environment, or it can be within ourselves. Unfortunately, most people look for their security, sometimes with obsession, from outside sources, rather than constructing their own solid, permanent foundation on which to stand.

- ✔ When our security is outside, we need to be pushed, pulled, praised and punished by others to move.
- ✔ When our security is inside us, we are driven by inner forces, and we function just as effectively when we receive power from without as when we don't.
- ✔ When our security is outside, we become high maintenance to others, constantly needing them to evaluate our performance and sometimes even our human worth!
- ✔ When our security is within, we have an internal point of evaluation and can correct and reinforce ourselves.

Externally motivated people aren't ever really sure how they feel, what they personally think about something or even how to act. But they know how to act to get someone else's approval. They are preoccupied with questions like:

- ✔ "Does everyone like me?"
- ✔ "Will they continue to like me forever?"
- ✔ "Will they still like me even long after I'm dead?"

They are dependent. And in those instances when there is mutual external approval, they are co-dependent.

It's nice to be liked, but it's unsettling when we have to sell our own inner security, our essence, who we really are, for the sake of our need to be liked and approved of by others. Ideally, and in reality, you are liked for who you really are, not for who you are pretending to be. When we are creating a new self for approval in each social situation, we experience tension.

The issues are not the real issues. The issue becomes approval. The most vital attitude nutrient you can acquire is INNER SECURITY, because you are sure you will always be solidly rooted in something consistent. Even in changing social environments, even in different countries, even in varying workplaces, you will always have you. And wherever you go, there you are!

Internally motivated people are driven by their own inner sources and inner forces. Their evaluation point is inside. When they receive compliments that their inner self knows aren't deserved, they aren't fooled by the fake words of others. Obviously, the inner secure person isn't easy prey for con artists who manipulate by falsely elevating egos. At times when no one notices their efforts, improvements, progress and contributions, they can still go forward — undeterred — because the inner secure person can reinforce himself or herself.

- ✔ Does the importance of inner security make sense to you?
- ✔ Does inner security feel right to you?
- ✔ Is there something you could do, today, to develop more inner security?

THERE IS ONLY ONE WAY OUT: THAT'S IN!

In his book *Flow* (1990), Mihaly Csikszentmihalyi records the insights he gathered from his study of the healthiest humans. On the subject of inner security versus environmental dependency, he encourages humans to draw from within. This is what the healthiest humans do. Commenting on the paradox that, despite our technological advancement today, we feel more helpless than our ancestors, the author writes:

> *There is no way out of this predicament than for the individual to take things in hand personally. If values and institutions no longer provide a framework as they*

once did, each person must use whatever tools are available to carve out a meaningful, enjoyable life. One of the most important tools is provided by psychology. Up to now, the most important contribution of this fledgling science has been to discover how past events shed light on one's current behavior. But there is another way this discipline of psychology can be put to use. It is helping us answer the question: Given that we are who we are, and with whatever hang-ups and repressions, what can we do to improve our future?

To overcome the anxieties and depressions of contemporary life, individuals must become independent of their social environment to the degree that they no longer respond exclusively in terms of its rewards and punishments. To achieve such an autonomy, a person has to learn to provide rewards to herself. She has to develop the ability to find enjoyment and purpose, regardless of external circumstances (p. 10).

INNER SECURITY IS THE PROCESS OF BECOMING A PERSON

In his book *On Becoming a Person* (1961), psychologist Carl Rogers describes the direction a growing person starts to take:

The individual increasingly comes to feel that the locus of evaluation lies within himself. Less and less does he look to others for approval or disapproval; for external standards to live by; for decisions and choices. He recognizes it rests within himself to choose; and the question

> *which matters is, "Am I living in a way which is deeply*
> *satisfying for me, and in a way which truly expresses*
> *me?" (p. 19)*

When feeling alone in the process of becoming a person, recognize that you are not alone. Others have taken the journey. Rogers adds:

> *El Greco must have realized as he looked at some of*
> *his early work that "good artists don't paint like that."*
> *But somehow he trusted his own inner experiencing of*
> *life, the process of himself, sufficiently that he could go*
> *on expressing his own unique perceptions. It was as*
> *though he could say, "Good artists do not paint like this,*
> *but I paint like this."*
> *...Einstein seems to have been unusually oblivious to*
> *the fact that good physicists did not think his kind of*
> *thoughts. Rather than drawing back on an inadequate*
> *academic preparation in physics, he simply moved toward*
> *being Einstein, toward thinking his own thoughts, toward*
> *being as truly and deeply himself as he could. This is not*
> *a phenomenon which occurs only in the artist or genius.*
> *Time and again, in my clients, I have seen simple people*
> *become significant and creative in their own spheres, as*
> *they developed more trust of the process going on within*
> *themselves, and have dared to feel their own feelings, and*
> *express themselves in their own unique way (p. 175).*

Turn inside to know. And to grow. Strangely, it is at those moments when you are not really alone at all, in a deeper way. You are with every other person who has taken the journey from being a carbon copy of someone else to becoming a person. One who stood for something.

- ✔ If you and I are totally alike, one of us becomes unnecessary.
- ✔ The way to really earn approval and respect is to be you.
- ✔ Stop overestimating others.
- ✔ Stop underestimating yourself.

THE MORE INNER SECURITY, THE LESS FEAR OF THE FUTURE

Take a little time to digest these two thoughts:

1. The more inner security I have, the less outer certainty I will need, because my certainty is within.
2. The less inner security I have, the more outer certainty I will need, because my certainty is outside of me.

INNER SECURITY NEW ATTITUDE NUTRIENT — ACQUISITION EXERCISES

Are you ready to start acquiring the attitudinal INNER SECURITY Nutrient? If so, remember to acquire it in the order of arrangement of your Dominant Attitude Style.

THINK

1. What are the three greatest achievement of your life?

    A.

    B.

    C.

    ✔ What qualities, assets, strengths and resources did those achievements require from you? (Name more than one for each.)

        A.

        B.

        C.

    ✔ These qualities are inside you. They are not fluff. They are real. On a small sheet of paper, list your three greatest achievements and the qualities you demonstrated you have.
    ✔ Fold the paper with your positive qualities on it, and put it in your wallet. Carry it with you and refer to it every time you need some **INNER SECURITY** Nutrients. (Soon you won't even need the paper, but for now do the exercise.)

2. Where in your life are you dependent upon reinforcement from outside?

   A.

   B.

   C.

   ✔ Make a plan for self-encouragement to build inner reinforcers so that you can increasingly build your inner security. What can you tell yourself to build your own security foundation?

3. List two times in your past when you were devastated by (A) lack of environmental support and (B) negative feedback:

   A.

   B.

   ✔ How would you handle those situations today after taking an INNER SECURITY Nutrient?

      A.

      B.

FEEL

1. Close your eyes and tell yourself a few meaningful times:
    ✔ "I have the inner resources to handle whatever I will experience."

2. What symbol do you feel or experience as something that represents strength? It can be anything from a mountain to sunshine, love, a rock, etc. Choose one that is meaningful to you at a feeling level.
    ✔ Close your eyes and imagine the strength symbol outside of you in the external world. Experience emptiness and weakness. Then slowly and consciously bring the symbol inside yourself and plant it permanently in your heart. As the symbol gets closer, feel yourself getting stronger and stronger.

3. What issues do you have feelings about that you haven't expressed because you suspect your personal view might not be acceptable?
    ✔ When appropriate go forward with your view, if the time feels right. Trust your inner knowing, and honestly share your feelings. You can be confident that it can't be wrong if this is the way you are personally feeling. Feelings are your personal facts. And you are the world's top expert on your feelings!

4. List some people you have positive feelings about whom you haven't told.

A.

B.

C.

✔ Call them up NOW and tell them your positive feelings for them. Feel your confidence developing as you express yourself. Remind yourself of your strength symbol in your heart.

DO

1. What is something positive you can do today that no one else will notice but you? Will you do it?
   ✔ Stand up and pat yourself on your back while congratulating yourself.
2. What do you want to do that nobody else has supported and you haven't done because of lack of support?
   ✔ Go do it. Get into it. Keep going under your own power!
3. Take action with the things that are right inside you. Where have you been acting dishonestly? Where have you not been true to yourself?
   ✔ Take action today to be true to your inner knowing.

INNER SECURITY NEW ATTITUDE NUTRIENT — ACQUISITION CHECK

Combine the three components of INNER SECURITY into one powerful you.

- ✔ Bring your INNER SECURITY thoughts and plans, your resources and assets, from your greatest achievements ever.
- ✔ Add your symbolic feeling of growing inner secure in your heart.
- ✔ Develop your action plan to go forward even without the applause of the crowd.
- ✔ Reinforce yourself with a pat on the back.

Do you think, feel and act as if your New Attitude Nutrient of INNER SECURITY is working for you now? Ask yourself the following three questions related to measuring the effectiveness of the INNER SECURITY Nutrient on your total attitude:

- ✔ Am I more focused on my inner assets, strengths and resources? (Thought)
- ✔ Am I feeling more secure in myself, more self-confident, more self-reliant and more trusting of my inner knowing? (Feeling)
- ✔ Am I taking self-determined actions, independent of outside support? (Action)

℞: ACCEPTANCE NUTRIENT

"Today, I'll condition myself to immediately accept anything I can't change!"　　*"What is, is!"*

Measuring the effectiveness of the ACCEPTANCE Nutrient for your life

- ✔ Nutrient to accept "what is, is," to focus energies constructively (Thought)
- ✔ Nutrient for acceptance, joy, serenity, calmness, peace, relaxation (Feeling)
- ✔ Nutrient to take action and "let go" or "let it be" (Action)

You will experience the effectiveness of the ACCEPTANCE Nutrient at that moment when you accept the things you can't change, feel calm about them and then move your energies on to change the things you want to change.

ACCEPTANCE Nutrients are produced to inhibit or protect against the development of the following common symptoms:

- ✔ anger at life
- ✔ bitterness
- ✔ blaming
- ✔ holding on to pain
- ✔ living in the past
- ✔ living with "shoulds," "oughts" and "musts"
- ✔ persecution complex
- ✔ stressed out

When used as recommended, you can expect growth in the following areas from ACCEPTANCE Nutrients:

- ✔ acceptance
- ✔ humorous approach to life
- ✔ letting go of the pain and the blame
- ✔ living joyfully with "what is"
- ✔ love
- ✔ peacefulness
- ✔ psychic freedom
- ✔ relaxation
- ✔ serenity

Just let go and the pain is gone — it's only with you because you have been holding on to it.

Is there something bothering you that you either can't do or haven't done anything to resolve? Is it zapping some of your mental and emotional energy? Decide how long you want this useless, draining intrusion in your life:

A. about a month
B. a year
C. the rest of my life
D. two more minutes

IMPORTANCE OF THE ACCEPTANCE NEW ATTITUDE NUTRIENT

Originally, humans thought the sun revolved around the earth and the earth was the center of the universe. Then we found out that we were not at the center because the earth revolved around the sun. This was so tough to take that many humans today have adopted a new theory of the universe. They believe that the universe revolves around them personally! This is called the "egocentric theory."

Have you ever met any of these egocentrists? Egocentrists believe that universal and earthly events revolve around them personally. You can observe egocentrists wherever you go. They stand out, of course. The universe has selected them personally to frustrate. Red lights, traffic jams, weather conditions, long lines in banks and supermarkets, IRS audits, and running out of gas are a few things that they have to go through. Others, like you and I, are in their way. We should know who they are and how important they are.

Now you and I, of course, are only rarely guilty of believing the egocentric philosophy of life. It is evidenced at those moments when we use the words "should" or "shouldn't" when describing how certain events in the universe should be arranged differently than they, in reality, are. There are no "shoulds" or "shouldn'ts" in the world. None. Where do they come from?

Well, if we were to run the universe, we would have to tell the universe what it should and shouldn't do, wouldn't we? Unfortunately, we get upset when the universe doesn't live up to our "should." And it should, shouldn't it?

There is another approach to life that is more practical, less frustrating and grandiose, while more therapeutic and simpler. Instead of living egocentrically with our "shouldy" demands, we can use our ACCEPTANCE New Attitude Nutrient and live with the clear fact that "What is, is!"

It really doesn't matter what should be, or what we wish would be, or what must be, or what ought to be, or what could have been or what is or isn't fair. Reality starts with "what is." And then it is up to us to change it if we don't like it. We change it with PURPOSE and PASSION, INNER SECURITY, ACCEPTANCE, UNDERSTANDING, COURAGE, INSPIRATION and LEADERSHIP.

It is ineffective and inaccurate to say, "Something shouldn't be the way it is." Why? Because it is the way it is! Isn't it?

Unfortunately, the average human uses over two hundred "shoulds" a day, and every single one produces only one thing: frustration. Make a tally of your "shoulds." You'll be amazed. Each time you say the word "should," excuse yourself to others by commenting, "Oh, I didn't tell you. I'm now in charge of the universe. That's why I'm telling the other five billion plus people what they should and shouldn't do!"

Lighten up! You'll find yourself laughing over things that used to drive you up a tree.

- ✔ The next time you go into a bank and notice that after you select the shortest line, the other lines start to move faster, you'll realize why. When you came into the bank, everyone secretly agreed that whichever line you chose, they, as a group, would work together to slow you up. Such is the burden of the egocentrist!
- ✔ You are in a restaurant, waiting for your meal to be served. You light up a cigarette, and your meal arrives after your first puff. The waitress was watching from the kitchen, waiting for you to light up just to frustrate you.

✔ You are on an airplane and your flight is delayed. A holdup for some no-good reason. You know your flight "should" be taking off. However, if you are late getting to the airport because of a prior universally arranged traffic jam, your flight, in that instance, is not delayed. It leaves on time and you miss it. You're frustrated. That's understandable because deep down you know that the airline, which flies to perhaps over four hundred cities, regulates its international flight schedule with one goal: to frustrate you personally!

ACCEPTANCE Nutrients may be able to add years to your life. And maybe more life to your years!

Remember these three precious words: What is, is!

ACCEPTANCE New Attitude Nutrient — Acquisition Exercises

THINK

1. Condition yourself to immediately accept anything you choose not to change. Ask yourself:
   ✔ Am I going to change this?
   ✔ If the answer is yes, make a plan, with a date for action.

✔ If the answer is no, then immediately accept it.

✔ Make a plan to find something you can change and change it.

✔ Rest assured mentally that you did get something done.

2. Find meaning in the things you can't change. Think of a major setback you experienced in your past.

   ✔ What was your first reaction to the setback?

   ✔ When you got your head together, what did you learn from the setback? Is this information you might never have acquired without the setback?

   ✔ Think of how you used that information after the setback to grow.

3. Is there an area of your life in which you are not seeing something clearly or perhaps have been fooling yourself about for a while?

   ✔ In your personal life, is a person giving you messages that you have not let in?

   ✔ Professionally, have you been slipping, but keep telling yourself, "Everything is okay?"

   ✔ Let this information in. Gain strength from it. Make a plan to get yourself back on track. You can do it!

4. Lighten up. Life is too important to take seriously.

   ✔ Recall a couple of stressful experiences which prove that the universe revolves around you personally, to the point that you find some humor in them.

5. Life isn't fair. Who said it was? Where in the world did we get such a crazy idea that life is fair?
   - ✔ Life isn't fair. Five billion out of the five and a half billion people living in the world today would trade places with you.
   - ✔ Life isn't fair. The average person in the world doesn't live to see thirty years of age. How old are you now?
   - ✔ Life isn't fair. If we hit ten red lights in a row, we might expect that the next ten lights be green. Don't bet on it!

FEEL

1. Think of something that is out of our control, but weighs down your heart.
   - ✔ Play some soft relaxing music.
   - ✔ Lay in a comfortable place.
   - ✔ Close your eyes.
   - ✔ Imagine yourself at the beach in the early morning with the wind blowing out to sea.
   - ✔ You have a huge kite and a beach bag. Put your problem into the beach bag, tie it to the kite and watch it float to the sky to Never Again Land.

DO

1. Make a list of some things from your past or present that you are helpless to change but you want to do something about.

   A.

   B.

   C.

   D.

   ✔ Take action, and "let it go!"
   ✔ Take a match and ceremoniously burn the list.

2. When you find yourself saying a "should" or a "shouldn't," quickly stop yourself, and ask instead, "What action am I going to take?"

ACCEPTANCE New Attitude Nutrient — Acquisition Check

Have fun, lighten up and use humor and relaxation. And remember, "What is, is!" Where in your life is the ACCEPTANCE Nutrient helping you already? You can measure the effectiveness of the ACCEPTANCE Nutrient by asking yourself the following three questions:

✔ Am I better able to accept what I can't change to use my energies to think of what can be changed? Does "What is, is!" make sense? (Thought)

✔ Do I find myself feeling more accepting, more joyful toward life in general, more serene, calmer, more peaceful, more relaxed? Does "What is, is!" feel right? (Feeling)

✔ Am I taking action? Am I "letting go" of the things I can't change? (Action)

New Attitude Nutrient #4

℞: UNDERSTANDING NUTRIENT

"Today, I'll proceed with understanding rather than judgment toward others!"

"Judging preaches to others. Understanding teaches us!"

Measuring the effectiveness of the UNDERSTANDING Nutrient for your life

- ✔ Nutrient to understand, rather than judge, to improve relationships and effectiveness with others (Thought)
- ✔ Nutrient for understanding, empathy, sensitivity, caring (Feeling)
- ✔ Nutrient to take action, using successful understanding skills (Action)

You will sense the effectiveness of the UNDERSTANDING Nutrient at that moment when you are feeling more understanding, less interpersonal tension and more effective relationships with others.

91

UNDERSTANDING Nutrients are produced to inhibit or protect against the development of the following common symptoms:

- ✔ anger at others
- ✔ bitterness
- ✔ conflict
- ✔ competing with others
- ✔ insensitivity
- ✔ interpersonal stress
- ✔ need to control others
- ✔ passive-aggressiveness
- ✔ preaching
- ✔ relationship problems

When used as recommended, you can expect growth in the following areas from UNDERSTANDING Nutrients:

- ✔ caring
- ✔ cooperating with others
- ✔ increased popularity
- ✔ improved relationships
- ✔ learning from others
- ✔ more effectiveness with people
- ✔ trusting others

SHOULDN'T OTHER PEOPLE BE MORE LIKE ME? JUDGING THEM WILL TEACH THEM HOW TO BE MORE LIKE ME

Mark Twain declared that "the first person in a conversation to draw a breath be declared the listener!" The world turns away from the preacher and turns toward the listener. Listening with empathy is the real secret of success with people.

Empathic understanding has been identified as the single most important human relations skills. Empathy is the desire, willingness, ability and skill to understand, rather than to judge, while listening to another. Empathy involves seeing from the eyes of another, thinking from the mind of another and feeling out of the heart of another. Empathy is truly walking a mile in the moccasins of another.

On the power of empathy, Harvard University professor Dr. Daniel Goleman recently discovered that our emotional intelligence is as vital for our practical success in life as our mental intelligence is. Two of the five components of emotional intelligence relate to our empathic connection with others: empathic acuity, or understanding another's feelings, and the skills for communicating our understanding of those feelings to another. The prime ingredient of the UNDERSTANDING New Attitude Nutrient is empathy. Empathic understanding of another is the opposite of judging another.

Psychologist Carl Rogers argues that judgment is the major barrier to understanding and communication. Rogers (1961) wrote:

> ...*the major barrier to mutual interpersonal communication is our very natural tendency to judge, evaluate, or approve or disapprove, the statements of the other person or group. Although this tendency to make evaluations is common in almost all interchanges of language, it is very much heightened in those situations where feelings and emotions are deeply involved. So the stronger our feelings, the more likely it is there will be no mutual element in communication. This tendency to react to any emotionally meaningful statement by forming an evaluation of it from our own point of view is, I repeat, the major barrier to interpersonal communication.*
>
> *But, is there any way of solving this problem, of avoiding this barrier? Real communication occurs, and this evaluative tendency is avoided, when we listen with understanding. What does that mean? It means to see the expressed idea and attitude from the other person's point of view, to sense how it feels to him, to achieve his frame of reference in regard to the thing he is talking about.*

Empathy isn't easy. In *The Brighter Side of Human Nature* (1990), Alfie Kohn wrote:

> ...*As George Herbert Mead saw it more than half a century ago "this putting of oneself in the places of others,*

> *this taking by one's self of their roles or attitudes, is not merely one of the various aspects or expressions of intelligence or intelligent behavior, but is the very essence of its character." A certain level of cognitive development is a prerequisite for being able to imaginatively take in the world from someone else's perspective, and this skill, in turn, has been shown to promote learning (p. 101).*

Kohn goes on to argue that empathic understanding involves not only (1) intelligence, (2) cognitive development and (3) imagination, but also (4) mental health, (5) flexibility, (6) openness and (7) generosity of spirit. Empathy, as you can see, is not for everyone. It is certainly not for the weak-willed or insecure. The UNDERSTANDING New Attitude Nutrient can give you the strength to let in the world of another, and to grow from it.

Remember: judging preaches to others; understanding teaches us.

IMPORTANCE OF THE **UNDERSTANDING** NEW ATTITUDE NUTRIENT

In ninety-five percent of conversations, when Person A is speaking, Person B, instead of really listening with understanding, is busy thinking things like, "Do I agree or disagree?" or "What should I say next?" And then, the one person in twenty who is extremely effective with people listens in a different way. This person listens to the other from the perspective of:

1. What is he or she thinking?
2. What is he or she feeling?
3. What actions will he or she probably take based upon his or her thoughts and feelings?

When Person A judges, instead of understands, Person B's communication, Person A may cut off a lot of potentially valuable and honest information. This is information from which Person A can learn, but the person misses the learning opportunity. Let's consider a number of disadvantages when we judge rather than listen to understand another.

1. We miss some information.
2. We frustrate the other person, who is unable to communicate the desired message to us without our judgmental interference.
3. We receive a distorted message, minus details that the speaker believes we don't want to hear or can't handle.
4. We hear inaccurate information because the other person tells us what he or she believes we want to hear.
5. We anger the other person when we judge, because he or she feels we are being condescending, judgmental and paternal.

No wonder a person who understands, rather than judges, becomes more effective with people. The communication becomes clean, clear, honest and enjoyable. The relationship becomes pleasurable and desirable.

There are ten ingredients or skills in the UNDERSTANDING New Attitude Nutrient:

1. *Welcoming skills* involve sensitively welcoming a new person, so he or she feels comfortable with you.
   - ✔ Smile and look the other person in the eye.
   - ✔ Shake the person's hand.
   - ✔ Get the person's name. Use his or her name frequently while smiling.
   - ✔ Result: the person feels welcome.

2. *Warmth skills* are your verbal and body language skills to communicate your genuine interest, caring and safety to another person.
   - ✔ Center on the other person's interests.
   - ✔ Communicate moment-to-moment involvement through your facial expressions.
   - ✔ Present yourself with open body language.
   - ✔ Block out all other distractions.
   - ✔ Be "with" the person.
   - ✔ Result: the person feels safe with you.

3. *Empathy skills* are the skills of listening to understand the feelings of another person, and then communicating those feelings back.
   - ✔ Listen to understand, not judge.

✔ Listen for feelings as well as facts.

✔ Accept the other person's complaints or disagreements.

✔ Share the feelings you felt and the words you heard.

✔ Accept without any strings attached.

✔ Result: the person feels understood by you.

4. *Mutuality skills* are the skills of finding common bonds, links and similarities between yourself and another person. The similarity-attraction principle states that "The more I feel and think you are similar to me, the more I like you, even if we just met."

✔ Listen closely to find things in common with the other person.

✔ Share your similarities.

✔ Use words like "we" or phrases like "people like us."

✔ Result: the person feels connected with you.

5. *Agreement skills* are the skills to create an agreement mood between yourself and another person.

✔ Structure your questions to get "yes" answers.

✔ Eliminate the disagreement word "but"; instead, condition yourself to use the agreement indicator "and."

✔ Result: the person feels united with you.

6. *Mirroring skills* are the skills of reflecting back the other person's body language, facial gestures and speed of speech.

✔ When the other person is expressive, mirror by becoming animated and expressive as well.

✔ When the other person speaks slowly or rapidly, mirror by speaking at the same pace.

✔ When you sense the other person wants to get closer, get closer. When you sense the person wants distance, back off a bit.

✔ Result: the person feels the two of you are in sync.

7. *Positioning skills* are the skills of consciously planting yourself solidly in a comfortable place in another person's mind and heart, so that the person can feel secure with you.

✔ Become a real open person, rather than a vague, elusive, fly-by-night phenomenon.

✔ Answer the other person's questions directly.

✔ Leave the other person with some real memory "tags" to grab hold of your name and important things about you.

✔ Reveal yourself without being overwhelming.

✔ Result: the person feels secure.

8. *Believability or credibility skills* are the skills of proving yourself trustworthy. You gain credibility by saying what you will do and then having it done by the time you said you would.

✔ Credibility = trustworthiness + knowledge.

✔ Trust is built by delivering.

✔ Result: people feel trust and respect.

9. *Personalizing skills* are the skills of re-humanizing rather than de-humanizing a person. Instead of being your nine o'clock appointment or a client, each person has a name and is unique and special.
   ✔ Notice something positive about the other person.
   ✔ Point out something unique about the person.
   ✔ Communicate your excitement about being with that person.
   ✔ If appropriate, give the person a positive nickname that is linked to a positive quality he or she possesses.
   ✔ Result: the person feels respected, significant, important and special.

10. *Enthusiasm skills* are the verbal and body language skills that communicate your excitement about another person.
   ✔ Listen with enthusiasm to the interests and concerns of the other person.
   ✔ Become animated about the other person's assets, strengths, hopes, dreams and goals.

UNDERSTANDING New Attitude Nutrient — Acquisition Exercises

THINK

1. Think of someone with whom you totally disagree on an issue. Use your understanding skills by leaving

your world, and see if you can build a case for the other person's opinion, reflecting, as accurately as possible, his or her viewpoint. See if you can do this empathic listening to the point where you almost understand his or her perspective!

2. Think of someone with whom you now have a disagreement. In your next conversation, be determined to use your UNDERSTANDING Nutrient.
    ✔ Listen for the person's thoughts.
    ✔ Listen for the person's feelings.
    ✔ Share your perception of the person's thoughts and feelings.
    ✔ Keep sharing until the person's eyes light up, the person's head starts nodding, the person stands closer and the person smiles.
    ✔ Resist the natural tendency to tell your side of the story, until the other person asks to hear it.

3. Think about a few of your friends. Determine whether each is a Think-er, Feel-er or Do-er. What would be the most effective way to use understanding skills with each of the three different dominant styles?
    ✔ Think-er
    ✔ Feel-er
    ✔ Do-er

FEEL

1. When in a disagreement with another person, stop feeling what you are feeling.

✔ If you were experiencing this person's emotions now, imagine what you would be feeling.

✔ Let those feelings pour out from your heart to his or hers.

2. Consider a close relationship you are in that has a lot of emotion. Instead of feeling how you feel about the other person, experience how he or she feels about you. Check out your perception with the person to sense if you are accurately sensing his or her feelings.

3. Give an "Understanding Party" to another person. For a whole luncheon, dinner or evening, use your understanding attitude and skills and keep reflecting the other person's feelings throughout your time together. There is little doubt that you will learn much more about this person's real feelings, undistorted, and you will feel a closeness in your relationship with him or her. You will also notice feelings of relief on the other person's part. Some people don't get this much understanding in a year.

DO

1. Memorize the ten understanding skills and constantly put them into practice:
    ✔ welcoming
    ✔ warmth
    ✔ empathy
    ✔ mutuality

- ✔ agreement
- ✔ mirroring
- ✔ positioning
- ✔ believability or credibility
- ✔ personalizing
- ✔ enthusiasm

2. Who are three people with whom you want to improve your relationship?

A.

B.

C.

Take action and decide which of the ten understanding skills you are going to use in your next conversation with each person you identified above.

UNDERSTANDING New Attitude Nutrient — Acquisition Check

Combine your total attitude of thinking, feeling and action to communicate your understanding of another person's total attitude. Begin mastering the extremely rewarding UNDERSTANDING Nutrient.

Measure the effectiveness of your UNDERSTANDING Nutrient by asking yourself three questions:

✔ Does it make sense to me that by understanding others, rather than judging them, they will be more comfortable and more honest with me and our communication will improve? (Thought)

✔ Am I feeling more understanding, empathy, sensitivity and caring for others if I allow myself to see the world through their eyes, feel the world from their heart and walk a mile in their shoes? (Feeling)

✔ Am I willing to take action in understanding and actually listen by using some of the understanding skills? (Action)

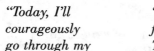

℞: COURAGE NUTRIENT

"Today, I'll courageously go through my anxieties and fears!"

"On the other side of your anxieties and fears is your New Attitude Growth Zone. The only way is through it. Today is your moment in time."

Measuring the effectiveness of the COURAGE Nutrient for your life

✔ Nutrient to bust through anxieties, fears and enter your New Attitude Growth Zone (Thought)
✔ Nutrient for courage, strength and will-ingness (Feeling)
✔ Nutrient to take action and move forward into the rich unknown possibilities (Action)

You will notice the COURAGE Nutrient working when you are facing your anxieties and fears with a full awareness that you are in the process of growing.

COURAGE Nutrients are produced to inhibit or protect against the development of the following common symptoms:

- ✔ anxiety
- ✔ discouragement
- ✔ fears
- ✔ living in "what was"
- ✔ overperfectionism
- ✔ retreating
- ✔ worries

When used as recommended, you can expect growth in the following areas from COURAGE Nutrients:

- ✔ courage
- ✔ determination to take action
- ✔ finding a way against all odds
- ✔ going forward — anyway!
- ✔ living to create what will be
- ✔ personal growth
- ✔ strength
- ✔ willingness to grow

What would you do if you had all the courage in the world? You do!

Finish the following sentence:

With a lot more courage, I would _____
_____!

✔ Is this goal important for you?
✔ Is this not the right time to go for this goal?
✔ When will be the right time to go for the goal?
✔ Will you have more courage at that point than you do now?

Three quick questions:

1. Think about the greatest achievement of your life. What was it? Relive it.
2. Was the greatest achievement of your life preceded by the greatest amount of anxiety in your life?
3. Where would you be today if you had let that harmless anxiety turn you back?

IMPORTANCE OF THE COURAGE NEW ATTITUDE NUTRIENT

Winston Churchill concluded that if he could have just one quality, it would be courage, because if he had courage, he could accumulate all the other qualities he needed. Throughout history, it has always been those leaders with courage who moved forward to make the world a better place. Courage is the unlimited quality that can get you over, under, around and through anything. Courage has been associated with strength, hope and love.

Our courage influences every area of our lives. Imagine:

- ✔ the courage to overcome our anxieties and fears
- ✔ the courage to be intimate with others
- ✔ the courage to act without guarantees
- ✔ the courage to be honest
- ✔ the courage to face our problems
- ✔ the courage to dream big, believe in oneself
- ✔ the courage to transcend our past and build our future
- ✔ the courage to give up addictions, compulsions and habits
- ✔ the courage to forgive and forget

The list goes on and on. Obviously, acquiring the COURAGE New Attitude Nutrient is going to have a dramatic impact on your life.

There are two specific COURAGE Nutrients to help you reach higher levels of success:

1. Developing "the courage to be imperfect"
2. Developing the courage to move through your anxieties to enter your New Attitude Growth Zone

DEVELOPING "THE COURAGE TO BE IMPERFECT!"

How long have you been working on becoming perfect? How close are you now?

Would you rather live a perfectly empty life or an imperfectly full one?

Psychologist Sofia Lazersfeld coined the beautiful and meaningful phrase "the courage to be imperfect!" What does the courage to be imperfect mean to you? Is it possible that the main thing that holds back our potential is the fear of making a mistake, doing something wrong, looking silly or failing?

With the courage to be imperfect, we proceed, not certain that we will be perfect, but certain that if we proceed, we will learn and grow.

Were not most of the great moments of your life moments when you stretched and reached for that new challenge? Uncertainty is the only cost we pay when we develop the courage to go forward anyway, imperfectly.

Think about it: the whole world opens up for you the moment you acquire the courage to be imperfect.

DEVELOPING THE COURAGE TO FLOW THROUGH YOUR ANXIETIES AND ENTER YOUR NEW ATTITUDE ZONE

Anxiety is a very scary word. There are many types of anxiety, and there are many effective medications to soften physiologically based anxiety. But we are talking about a different form of anxiety here: anxiety that is psychologically based in our struggle between growing into our New Attitude Growth Zone versus stagnating in the safe, predictable area of our Comfort Rut Zone.

Anxiety is a butterfly-ish feeling of uncertainty. It is the thought and accompanying feelings that something terrible is going to happen and we have no control over it. (Anxiety is different from a fear, because the danger is very specific in a fear.)

I'd like you to think about anxiety a little differently. I call anxiety "growth pains." Philosopher Soren Kierkegaard called anxiety "the cutting edge of change." Think of anxiety as "uncertainty," but uncertainty doesn't mean bad, does it? Uncertainty means probably different. That means there is a chance things will be worse, but there is also, although rarely mentioned, a chance things will be dramatically better!

Humans think the unknown is scary.

- ✔ In the time of Columbus, maps of the unknown world had pictures of serpents. Imagine, the United States of America once was viewed as being infested with serpents!
- ✔ Remember the old science fiction movies with odd-shaped, scary characters from the planet Mars who wanted to destroy Earth and all us Earthlings? Have you seen any Martians on the recent close-ups of Mars? I haven't!

It's the same way with our lives. When faced with choosing a growth opportunity filled with uncertainty or choosing certainty that is stagnating, begin thinking of the positive possibilities by choosing growth over stagnation. Push yourself forward by thinking about what you will learn by going forward that you would miss by retreating. Because something is unknown and produces anxiousness, begin thinking that the unknown can actually be good. If you walk down the rich, unknown path, you may find things you never saw before that can enrich your life. Hasn't it always been that way before for you? Haven't some of the richest moments of your life been those moments when you chose growth over stagnation?

Remember: Nothing ventured, nothing gained.

Let's look at anxiety this way:

The thin line between your Old Attitude Comfort Rut Zone and your New Attitude Growth Zone is called anxiety. *You have to go through your fear or anxiety to grow into your new attitude zone.* You can't pick up the security and certainty of the first-base bag as you run to second base. But remember, the run doesn't count until you touch all the bases. You can't stay on first forever.

Your comfort zone soon becomes your rut zone. You need to grow to stay one step ahead of stagnation. Remember, every great achievement in your life was preceded by great amounts of anxiety. *Flow through your anxiety.* Take the direct route through the anxiety and enter your New Attitude Growth Zone of unlimited possibilities. There are no serpents or Martians.

Don't let that little thin line hold you back. Take your courage to be imperfect and bust through your anxieties and fears and come alive again. At this moment. While you have it!

COURAGE New Attitude Nutrient — Acquisition Exercises

Remember to proceed with your Dominant Attitude Style first.

THINK

1. Start to develop the courage to be imperfect. In what areas of your life do you need to have more courage?
    ✔ Personal life?
    ✔ Social life?
    ✔ Professional life?

2. What are some of the things you have achieved that were once in your New Attitude Growth Zone but you busted through to master? Those things are now in your old attitude Comfort Rut Zone. Take a COURAGE Nutrient and continue to grow.

3. Think of some area of your life where you really want to expand.
    ✔ What is the worst thing that can happen to you if you grow?
    ✔ What is the best thing that can happen to you if you grow?
    ✔ What will happen to you if you don't choose growth?

4. Where are your limits in your New Attitude Growth Zone?
    ✔ Have you ever broken through your limits before? Are there things you can do today that you never dreamed you could ever do?
    ✔ Well, guess what. There are things that you think you can't do today that you will be doing tomorrow. With courage!

FEEL

1. What would you really like to experience or accomplish but are anxious, tense or afraid to take action?
    - ✔ Turn your anxious feelings into feelings of excitement.
    - ✔ Focus on all of the great feelings you will have — the exhilaration as you bust through that little thin line.
    - ✔ Get excited about your possibilities, knowing that in a short period of time you'll be renewing yourself and growing.
    - ✔ Associate staying in your comfort zone with being stuck in a rut.
    - ✔ Eliminate those stuck feelings and focus on positive possibilities.
    - ✔ Want it bad, in the heart.

DO

1. As you look at the circle of your Comfort Rut Zone and your New Attitude Growth Zone, write in some areas of your life that are in your comfort zone (for example, maybe sports). Then list some things that are in your New Attitude Growth Zone. The less comfortable you are with an area of your life, draw that area farther away from your Comfort Rut Zone, in your New Attitude Growth Zone.

✔ Choose one goal in your New Attitude Growth Zone. What actions can you take today to move toward entering your New Attitude Growth Zone?

A.

B.

C.

2. What can you "not do"? Conquer it! Take action with the courage to be imperfect and stretch yourself.

COURAGE NEW ATTITUDE NUTRIENT — ACQUISITION CHECK

What one thing are you going to do with courage, starting now?

Measure the effectiveness of the COURAGE Nutrient by asking yourself the following three questions:

✔ Does it make sense to me that I grow by going through my fears and anxieties because I gain knowledge, information and feedback I would not have if I stayed in my rut zone? (Thought)
✔ Do I feel more strength, more courage and more excitement for growing? (Feeling)

✔ Am I taking action and going forward into the rich treasures hidden in the unknown unlimited universe? (Action)

℞: INSPIRATION NUTRIENT

"Today, I'll act out of my spirit, not my ego!"

"Flowing from my universal energy gets better results than acting out of my selfish ego!"

Measuring the effectiveness of the INSPIRATION Nutrient for your life

✔ Nutrient to transcend ego, find universal, not self-ish, perspective (Thought)
✔ Nutrient for inspiration, energy, expansion, positive motivation (Feeling)
✔ Nutrient to take action with universal base (Action)

You will sense the effectiveness of the INSPIRATION Nutrient in those moments when you resist the tendency to act out of your limited ego, and instead are moved by your unlimited universal creative spirit.

INSPIRATION Nutrients are produced to inhibit or protect against the development of the following common symptoms:

- ✔ closed-minded
- ✔ creative blockage
- ✔ defensiveness
- ✔ ego-centered
- ✔ fatigue
- ✔ neighborhood view of the universe
- ✔ pessimism
- ✔ sadness
- ✔ selfishness

When used as prescribed, you can expect growth in the following areas from INSPIRATION Nutrients:

- ✔ energized
- ✔ expanding
- ✔ feeling of being at home in the universe
- ✔ open-minded
- ✔ optimism
- ✔ positive motivation
- ✔ unlimited creativity
- ✔ universal view of the universe

NOTHING IS BIGGER THAN YOU: YOU ARE THE UNIVERSE!

Would you respond differently to a big, unexpected bill if you had all the financial resources in the world instead of only the money that was in your pocket at that moment?

Would you respond differently to personal criticism if you were drawing from the unlimited, creative resources of the universe than if you were operating out of your own limited ego?

IMPORTANCE OF THE INSPIRATION NEW ATTITUDE NUTRIENT

When we put ourselves into our most resourceful state, we are infinitely more creatively capable than when we are drawing from our limited time, space and body state. Investigation into this miraculous nutrient was begun after psychologist-philosopher Wayne Dyer initiated study on the detrimental effects of ego in his book, *Your Sacred Self*. The INSPIRATION New Attitude Nutrient is designed to produce an immediate attitude transformation, one whose vantage point on life rises from self to universal.

Imagine having the ability to handle stress by empowering your thought, feeling and action states with greater strength and creative energy. Consider a whole range of models from which you can choose to operate as you flow through life. On the one hand, you can move from the near-depleted resources present in your smallest possible frame of reference, that is, your ego. At the other end of your continuum of potential resources, you can extract the strength from your universal, unlimited, spirit state.

Let's compare the relative capacity, force and vitality present in each of the two extremes:

Ego State	*Spirit State*
critical	inspirational
threatened	embraces
physical form	boundless energy
limited to time	timeless reference
limited to place	universal
defends	creates
maintenance	enhancement
disease model	wellness, potential model
fatigues	regenerates
self-conscious	spontaneous
doubts or believes	knows
restricts	empowers
takes, consumes	gives, creates
hesitates	flows
uses the moment as means to an end	uses the moment as an end in itself

Picture the ego state as closing you up, while the spirit state opens you up to new resources within yourself — the universe in your mind and heart. Consider a few of the major changes that occur when you transform yourself from ego to spirit:

1. Transforming myself from critical ego to inspiration spirit produces in me a sensation of not judging myself, but rather inspiring myself.

2. Transforming myself from being threatened by outside forces to embracing and incorporating those outside forces allows me to absorb and grow from an experience, rather than close myself off from it because of being threatened.

3. Transforming myself from physical form to boundless energy gives me the realization that I am more than my body and my physical possessions. I will live on long after my physical body withers away, just as those whose energies have touched my life live on in my spirit even after their body forms pass. If something can move something or someone else, it is proof of its existence.

4. Transforming myself from the boundaries of this moment in time to a timeless reference point allows me to draw resources, strengths and insights from a universal time perspective.

5. Transforming myself and my thinking from this limited vantage point, this neighborhood place, to a new vantage point, the universe, I gain resources I

was never aware of before. Yet, I can do this without leaving my neighborhood. I don't have to go somewhere else in the world to understand; I only have to go somewhere else in my world to understand. The universe is within.

6. Transforming myself from defending my closed up ego to creating from my opened up spirit expands me to as large as my universal mind.

7. Transforming my ego from a maintenance, protection mode to an enhancement mode enlarges me and grows me to actualize, not just survive.

8. Transforming myself from a disease model of me (What's wrong here?) to a wellness and spiritual potential model (What is possible!) changes my focus and the very questions I ask myself in life.

9. Transforming my ego, which gets fatigued under stress, to mobilizing my universal resources to regenerate my energies renews rather than fatigues me.

10. Transforming my self-conscious ego to become universally aware takes the pressure off my efforts and performance. I'm too busy creating out of my spontaneity to notice and judge me.

11. Transforming myself from doubting or believing to knowing gives me the certainty to move forward.

12. Transforming myself from restrictions because of my limited physical ego to empowering myself with deeper powers enlarges my awareness of my already-there universe.

13. Transforming myself from a taking and consuming motivation, to nourish and feed my ego, to a giving and creating motivation enables me to feel my impact on the external world.

14. Transforming myself from a hesitation state to a "flow" mode allows me to get more out of each moment. Without a doubt.

15. Transforming myself from using this moment as a means to an end to using it as an end in itself enables me to find rewards now, not later.

Let's consider these last two points, "flow" and "moments as ends," individually to better understand how the INSPIRATION Nutrient will enrich your life.

Flow!

"Flow" is a word used by Mihaly Csikszentmihalyi in his book of the same name. The author concluded that for 2,300 years, since Aristotle asked the question, "What is happiness?" no answer could be found. But he argues that we have now found what happiness is.

Happiness is the state of being totally absorbed in a task. This is when we are in a flow. Flow improves the quality of that experience and provides increased enjoyment, concentration and involvement. In flow, the sense of time and self-consciousness disappears, and a feeling of transcendence and breaking out of boundaries appears.

Flow is the state of being so absorbed in an activity that nothing else seems to matter. The immersion in the experience itself takes the focus away from self-consciousness and outside problems.

Curiously, happiness is not something that happens or something that power can command. It does not depend upon outside events, but rather how we interpret them. Happiness is a condition that must be prepared for and cultivated by each of us privately. People who learn to control their inner experiences are able to determine the quality of their lives.

Using This Moment as an End in Itself

Imagine. Some students take a college course to get a degree to get a job to make money to retire early! Most of our lives, we are doing something now because it will lead to a reward later. When you think about it, most of our valuable two and a half billion life instants are lost and consumed as moments that are mere means to another end. Another moment later, some time in the possible future, will be the good one.

When we are using our INSPIRATION New Attitude Nutrient, we are experiencing this moment, now, as an exciting end in itself. We are taking that college course in the spirit of excitement for what we are learning, now, at this moment. Our degree will follow anyway, especially if we stay inspired by the powerful findings unleashed in this moment. But our source of motivation is not the degree. We are taking the course for the knowledge we are acquiring now.

Where could you flow from your spirit and attach more meaning to those precious seconds of your life that may pass you by, as mere servants, or secondary citizens, of your day?

INSPIRATION New Attitude Nutrient — Acquisition Exercises

THINK

1. Think of the last time you were criticized by someone. How did you respond to the criticism? Reread the fifteen differences between ego state and spirit state. Imagine the wide range of potential responses to the same criticism, based upon your smaller or larger frame of reference.
   - ✔ Respond to the criticism from an ego state.
   - ✔ Respond to the same criticism from a spirit state.
   - ✔ What thoughts, feelings and future actions were generated by each state?
2. Think of some overwhelming challenges you face.
   - ✔ Respond from an ego state and think of the big challenges and the small you (ego).

✔ Respond to the same challenge from a universal, unlimited spirit, flow state.
✔ Break the tasks down into manageable units. Get fully immersed, flowing, totally absorbed in the first, then the second, etc. Will you find this way more fun and effective?

3. Remember:
   ✔ Think inspirational
   ✔ Think boundless energy
   ✔ Think timeless reference
   ✔ Think spontaneous
   ✔ Think flow
   ✔ Think of the power in this moment

FEEL

1. Close your eyes. Transform your feelings and yourself from the following limitations:
   ✔ This place
   ✔ This time
   ✔ My body
   ✔ My age
   ✔ My job
   ✔ My background
   ✔ My way of thinking

2. Put yourself into a state of flow now. Take a routine boring task and get fully absorbed in it.

✔ Experience the task with all of your senses.

✔ Imagine how this process is making the world different.

✔ Create some ways of making the task more fun and more efficient.

3. Consider some people in your life with whom your relationship might be stagnant.

✔ Renew by recalling some earlier, exciting times.

✔ Generate your feelings by remembering all the things these people have done for you through the years.

DO

1. What is a current challenge you are facing?

✔ Reread the differences between the ego and spirit states.

✔ What actions could you take now toward the challenge by transforming yourself into a spirit state?

2. Where in your life are you hesitating in taking action?

✔ Put yourself into a state of flow.

✔ Move forward, not with a long-term goal in mind, but rather with a desire to use the moment as an end in itself.

✔ Enjoy the process of life. It's all we have!

INSPIRATION NEW ATTITUDE NUTRIENT — ACQUISITION CHECK

How has the INSPIRATION New Attitude Nutrient helped you grow? Can you name one or two specific ways in which you are different after learning the contrast between ego state and spirit state?

Measure the effectiveness of the INSPIRATION Nutrient by asking yourself three questions:

✔ Does it make sense to me that if I draw from my unlimited creative mind, I will have more information resources than if I act out of my limited ego? (Thought)
✔ Do I feel inspired, energetic, expansive and positive motivation when I experience the unlimited, universal, creative energy I have inside me? (Feeling)
✔ Am I taking action out of a foundation that is bigger than my limited self? (Action)

℞: LEADERSHIP NUTRIENT

"Today, I'll take the lead in changing the world!"

"One person with a dream becomes a majority in any size group!"

Measuring the effectiveness of the LEADERSHIP Nutrient for your life

- ✔ Nutrient to communicate respect and vision and encourage buy-in (Thought)
- ✔ Nutrient for enthusiasm, confidence, optimism and high energy (Feeling)
- ✔ Nutrient to motivate others to unite and to move toward goals (Action)

You will sense the effectiveness of the LEADERSHIP Nutrient in those moments you are able to mobilize yourself and others to think, feel and take action to improve the quality of life in your world.

LEADERSHIP Nutrients are produced to inhibit or protect against the development of the following symptoms:

- ✔ decision-making difficulties
- ✔ helplessness
- ✔ feelings of inferiority
- ✔ joining cliques against progress
- ✔ part of the problem
- ✔ passive complainer
- ✔ resenting others, especially leaders
- ✔ shyness

When used as recommended, you can expect growth in the following areas from LEADERSHIP Nutrients:

- ✔ encourager to others
- ✔ momentum-maker
- ✔ mover and shaker
- ✔ motivator to others
- ✔ inspiring others to take action
- ✔ part of the solution
- ✔ respect for and belief in others
- ✔ responsibility
- ✔ self-confidence
- ✔ visionary

BE THE CHANGE YOU WANT TO SEE IN THE UNIVERSE!

Psychologist Abraham Maslow would ask his classes at Brandeis University each year:

- ✔ "Who in this room is going to become the great American leader?"
- ✔ "Who in this room is going to bring about world peace?"
- ✔ "Who in this room is going to be the great American president?"

Year after year, no one would raise a hand. Instead, each individual would look around at the others and wonder if the "great one" was in the room that day. Perhaps some day they could brag that their claim to fame was that they once were in a class with someone who really made something of himself or herself.

And then Maslow would look at one person and say, "If not you, then who?"

You don't have to have the job title of leader to be a leader. In fact, some people who hold job titles as leaders aren't! Whenever you are motivating, encouraging or inspiring others, you are a leader. *A leader is the one on the team or in the family who has the greatest desire to make something happen and has the least desire for credit when it happens.*

IMPORTANCE OF THE **LEADERSHIP** NEW ATTITUDE NUTRIENT

A dream calls out for someone to fulfill it. Leaders are those who respond and mobilize the people around them.

Your LEADERSHIP Nutrient will help you become inspired and offer you some practical skills in motivating others to help reach that collective purpose.

Mark Twain observed that everyone talks about the weather, but nobody ever does anything about it. Like the weather, everyone talks about unmotivated people. But, unlike the weather, there is something we can do about it. You can be the motivating leader who is a positive influence on the lives of those around you.

- ✔ You can empower others to build a dream and motivation by helping them develop purpose and passion. (PURPOSE & PASSION)
- ✔ You can encourage the development of inner security by giving them room to meet their challenge driven by inner security. (INNER SECURITY)
- ✔ You can help them avoid frustration by immediately accepting the things they can't change and using their creative energies wisely elsewhere. (ACCEPTANCE)
- ✔ You can invite them to work together through mutual understanding and respect for each person's unique contribution to the team. (UNDERSTANDING)
- ✔ You can encourage them to think big; go through their doubts, fears and anxieties together; and move into their new attitude zone. (COURAGE)
- ✔ You can inspire them to rise above acting from their egos and move from their universal spirit. (INSPIRATION)

When you make a full commitment to become a positive force, at that moment you acquire a huge advantage over pessimistic leaders. The advantage is that no human achievement has ever occurred because of pessimism or cynicism. Every monumental accomplishment — from placing the flag on the moon to curing polio — was the result of the efforts of optimistic, motivated people who were inspired by someone to go on, go on and who refused to quit even in the temporary darkness of nighttime. You can be the motivating leader who empowers by shining the spotlight on your team's possibilities.

Interpersonal Leadership Skills

1. Leading through Effective Communication
   A. Developing your leadership attending skills
      - ✔ Good eye contact
      - ✔ A relaxed, non-distracting body posture
      - ✔ Stay on the other person's topic
      - ✔ Strive to understand 100% of a person's message
   B. Developing your skills in listening
      - ✔ Focus on feelings and emotions of others
      - ✔ Target a person's concerns
      - ✔ Use non-judgmental listening at first
   C. Developing your skills in responding to others' communications

✔ Use "door-openers," such as "Can you tell me more about...?"

✔ Avoid shoot-and-reload dialogue (preparing what you are going to say when the other person is speaking)

✔ Respond non-judgmentally

✔ Communicate your understanding of the other person's message

2. Motivating People through Encouragement

   A. Developing your responsibility and productivity skills

      ✔ Focus on efforts, progress and contributions

      ✔ Recognize assets, resources and potential

      ✔ Hold people responsible without blaming them

      ✔ Identify the moment a person is turned off

      ✔ Energize your personal enthusiasm for a person's joys

   B. Developing your respect for others

      ✔ Convey, "I have confidence in you"

      ✔ Understand the importance of your positive expectations

      ✔ Focus on their interests

      ✔ Recognize the other person's "claims to fame"

      ✔ Respect people by not interfering

      ✔ Cooperate, don't compete

      ✔ Build relationships with mutual respect

✔ Recognize the value of differences and uniqueness
✔ Identify similarities
✔ Develop your sense of humor

LEADERSHIP New Attitude Nutrient — Acquisition Exercises

THINK

1. Where in your life does a group of people you are with need a leader?
    ✔ Make a commitment to get the group mobilized.
    ✔ Help develop a joint dream.
    ✔ Point out the strengths and assets of everyone who will help reach that dream.
    ✔ Show each person the benefits the dream has for him or her.
    ✔ Focus on effort, improvement and progress.
    ✔ Celebrate together.
2. To whom in your life could you communicate more respect?
3. Who needs you now to point out their strengths, assets and resources?
4. Who needs some inspiration or some passion and purpose?
5. Make a list of goals, with achievement dates.

FEEL

1. In which area of your life are you in a rut which is putting others into a rut as well?
   - ✔ Renew your feelings, regenerating your excitement for the job.
   - ✔ Fire up your feelings by finding new ways of looking at the same old thing.
2. Constantly monitor the feelings of the others on your team.
   - ✔ Each individual member
   - ✔ The team's overall feelings
3. Inspire your team members by speaking from your heart when talking to them. You'll mobilize their energies!

DO

1. When taking action with the team, motivate by understanding each person's Dominant Attitude Style and moving him or her from that Dominant Attitude Style.
   - ✔ Think-er
   - ✔ Feel-er
   - ✔ Do-er
2. Focus on the actions taken:
   - ✔ Notice efforts
   - ✔ Notice improvements
   - ✔ Notice progress
   - ✔ Notice contributions
   - ✔ Notice those who cooperate unselfishly

LEADERSHIP NEW ATTITUDE NUTRIENT — ACQUISITION CHECK

Somebody has to be the leader. In what areas of your life is it important for you to take charge to influence others to grow and to help yourself to grow?

Measure the effectiveness of the LEADERSHIP Nutrient by asking yourself three questions:

- ✔ Does it make sense that if I communicate respect for others ("I believe in you!") and vision ("We have an important purpose!"), I am more likely to encourage others to buy-in to new dreams? (Thought)
- ✔ Do I feel my enthusiasm, confidence, higher energy and greater optimism? (Feeling)
- ✔ Am I taking action to get others to take action? (Action)

If not you, then who?

And if not TODAY, then when?

Always remember: TODAY is your best chance to change your life!

CLOSING THOUGHTS

Two billion five hundred million moments of power in just one lifetime. Imagine that! If New Attitude Nutrients give you more pleasure, power or purpose in any one of those moments, consider the possibilities!

I trust and hope that you have grown through your New Attitude Nutrients. You can now manufacture your own. When you see a quality you need, write it down and keep it — and develop it.

Remember, when things seem aimless or purposeless, take PURPOSE & PASSION.

When things seem out of your control, take INNER SECURITY.

When things are frustrating, take ACCEPTANCE.

When you're upset with someone or feeling intolerant, take UNDERSTANDING.

When you're anxious or tense, take COURAGE.

When you're down on yourself, take some INSPIRATION.

And when a group of people need to come to life, take LEADERSHIP.

And most importantly — Do it TODAY!

REFERENCES

Ansbacher, Heinz and Rowena Ansbacher. *The Individual Psychology of Alfred Adler.* New York: Basic Books, 1956.

Csikszentmihalyi, Mihaly. *Flow: The Psychology of Optimal Experience.* New York: Harper & Row, 1990.

Dinkmeyer, Don and Lewis Losoncy. *The Skills of Encouragement.* Boca Raton, Florida: St. Lucie Press, 1996.

Dyer, Wayne. *Your Sacred Self.* New York: HarperCollins, 1995.

Ellis, Albert. *Reason and Emotion in Psychotherapy.* Secaucus, New Jersey: Lyle-Stuart, 1973.

Ellis, Albert. Changing Rational-Emotive Behavior Therapy (RET) to Rational Emotive Behavior Therapy (REBT). *The Behavior Therapist,* Vol. 16, No. 10, Winter 1993.

Ellis, Albert and Robert Harper. *A New Guide to Rational Living.* Hollywood, California: Wilshire Books, 1975.

Goleman, Daniel. *Emotional Intelligence.* New York: Bantam, 1995.

Kohn, Alfie. *The Brighter Side of Human Nature.* New York: Basic Books, 1990.

Losoncy, Lewis. *Turning People On*. New York: Simon & Schuster, 1977.

Losoncy, Lewis. *The Motivating Team Leader*. Boca Raton, Florida: St. Lucie Press, 1995.

Losoncy, Lewis and Diane Losoncy. *What Is, Is!* Boca Raton, Florida: St. Lucie Press, 1997.

Maslow, Abraham. *Motivation and Personality*. New York: Harper & Row, 1954.

Maslow, Abraham. *The Farther Reaches of Human Nature*. New York: Viking Press, 1971.

Rogers, Carl. *On Becoming a Person*. Boston: Houghton-Mifflin, 1961.

Sternberg, Robert J. *Successful Intelligence*. New York: Simon & Schuster, 1996.